THE
PROPERTY
BOOK

THE
PROPERTY
BOOK

ANN MAURICE

with KATE FAULKNER

First published in 2004 by Collins
An imprint of HarperCollins*Publishers*
77–85 Fulham Palace Road, London, W6 8JB

everything clicks at: www.collins.co.uk

Text © Talkback Productions Ltd 2004
For a detailed breakdown of photography credits, see page 192

Project manager: Emma Callery
Designer: Bob Vickers

For HarperCollins:
Senior managing editor: Angela Newton
Art direction: Luke Griffin
Editor: Alastair Laing
Editorial assistant: Lisa John
Production controller: Chris Gurney

A CIP catalogue record for this book is available from the British Library

ISBN 0007175507

Colour reproduction by Colourscan
Printed and bound in Great Britain by Bath Press

CONTENTS

INTRODUCTION

For those of you who are unfamiliar with my background, you might be interested to know that prior to my career in interior design and TV's House Doctor I was a realtor (that's 'American' for estate agent) in California for 13 years. Over the years I learnt a great deal about the intricacies of buying and selling property. And there were plenty. Since then, my six-year involvement in Britain as TV's House Doctor has brought me face to face with the property market in the UK ... and I am still constantly amazed by the differences.

In California, as realtors, we are required to be licensed by the state before being able to work. We have to pass a very arduous competency test and many of us have university qualifications and are well respected. The realtor's job description is much broader than that of a UK estate agent. We interview the buyer, show them around prospective properties, write the contract and present it to the seller and handle all negotiations. As the seller's agent, the realtor acts strictly on their behalf to ensure they are justly represented. There is no such thing as 'gazumping' and the laws are much stricter to protect both the buyer and seller. It is the realtor's job to do everything in their power to ease the stress and strain of buying and selling. Of course, the realtors' commissions are generally much higher than those of UK estate agents.

In comparison, in the UK most estate agents make little money. Their commissions are less than a third of those earned by US realtors. The buying/selling process takes months longer in Britain, mainly because of the time from offer to exchange. Furthermore, the entire process is much more uncertain. So, having now spent some time learning about the UK property market, I feel it's time to write a book that combines this knowledge with those 'tried and true' real estate techniques brought with me from California.

This book is a comprehensive, useful and practical guide to buying and selling, offering a fresh approach to moving home from start to finish. Included are detailed step-by-step guides to the process of buying and selling as well as checklists to assist you with all the things you need to consider or remember. At the end of each section there are guides to help when things go wrong and contact details for organisations that can help if you feel you need independent support for progressing any complaints.

When moving home in the UK, the key to a smooth move is to understand every step of how to get from your current property to the new one. You need to know how to choose the right estate agent, conveyancer and other services. It is a complicated process and if things go wrong you need to know what you can do about it and who can help.

This book will help you through the process, no matter if you are a seasoned or first-time buyer, buying to let, property developer or planning for your retirement. For on-going help and support you can visit my website (www.housedoctor.co.uk) where you will find all the latest information on buying and selling and links to companies mentioned in this book, plus many more that I think you would find useful.

Hopefully after reading this book, you might even find buying and selling an exciting and enjoyable experience. Good luck!

ANN MAURICE

SECTION ONE

SELLING
YOUR HOME

When deciding to sell your home, ensure you are armed with as much information as possible and understand what type of market you are selling in. This section covers everything you need to know, from researching the market and finding the best estate agent to understanding what can help you sell your home, even in a slow market.

But the work doesn't stop once you have received an offer. You then need to make sure you have chosen your buyer carefully, that you understand every step of the legal process and how long each step should take. In this section we explain these steps to help ensure you can be prepared and enjoy a smooth move.

WHY SELL YOUR HOME?

The decision to sell one's home is not one that is usually made lightly or on the spur of the moment. It is a major decision that can often be forced on you by changing circumstances – welcome or not. Getting married, starting or expanding a family, relocating for work, or watching the family downsize as children leave home can all be reasons, as can difficult circumstances such as death, divorce or loss of income. Of course, some people move for less apparent life-changing reasons – maybe they just want more space, a nicer environment or just feel it's time to try somewhere new. But whatever the reason, happy or sad, the actual life-changing occurrences that prompt the sale are stressful enough on their own without the added tensions of house buying and selling.

This book is filled with information to make sure the process is as easy and enjoyable as possible. If you feel in control of what happens – whatever the circumstances of the move – you are more likely to find the entire transition less of a strain and more manageable. Even if things don't go quite according to plan, you will find that my hints and tips will help you to get things back on track – and hold on to your sanity.

Amazingly, almost half the numbers of people who start off buying or selling end up stopping the process. One good reason for staying put is that your home is actually better than you thought. With some improvement it's a much more cost-effective (and painless) way of achieving the desired effect without the enormous outlay of cash and effort.

Unfortunately, many find that when they come to buy or sell their property — particularly if their financial circumstances have changed — they simply can't find anywhere else they can afford or someone to buy their house.

In Britain estate agents do not charge for helping you look for a property; they only get paid when someone sells — and when that sale is

To start the process of selling your home, the first question you need to ask yourself is – do you really want to leave the home you have been living in?

final. So they have an incentive to encourage people to look around. It also doesn't cost you anything to put your property up for sale or to put in an offer on another property. You only have to cough up the cash at the exchange and, naturally, at the final sale.

So, the real question you need to ask yourself before you start the process is whether or not you want (or need) to make the effort to buy or sell. If you decide the answer is a resounding 'Yes', we can help you. Remember, the more research and planning you put in, both in selling and buying, the less problematic and stressful the process is likely to be.

MOVE OR IMPROVE?

To move or not to move ... that is the question. Is it going to be easier and less costly to improve your existing property or do you really need to bite the bullet and desert the homestead?

If you're moving because you need more space — an extra bedroom, study or bathroom, for example — you might be able to create the

needed space within your existing property through a loft or garage conversion or extension. Before you can make this decision, however, you need to get a quote for the costs and make sure there are no planning permission problems likely to pop up — such as a neighbour objecting to the enlargement of your property. It is also a good idea to remind yourself that the extension or conversion won't happen overnight. You're likely to be living in a building site for some time and that brings its own stresses and strains.

QUICK TIP

Don't forget that the legal costs for leasehold and freehold property can differ significantly as the legal procedures are more complex and involve a third party, the leaseholder.

Once you've done the calculations (see below), you can make a decision based on comparable costs: building vs moving. While you're deciding, don't forget to find out if the home improvement will add value to your property in the longer term, too. You can do this by asking a local estate agent or surveyor, who can usually give you a good idea of how much the changes will add to your property's worth.

SURVEY YOUR ORIGINAL SURVEY

If you've kept the original survey done on the property when you bought it, run through the main points to see if you forgot to make any of the recommended changes. Decide whether you want to carry out any outstanding work or leave it to the new owners. But remember, it may mean the sale price is lower than you expect.

THE COST OF MOVING

You need to think about various costs involved in selling your property. This isn't difficult and can easily be broken down into 'must spend' and 'possibles and probables'. The list will vary depending on the type of property, the selling price and the company that you use to move home.

You will then need to budget for everything that is individual to you such as: cleaning, fixes, storage and any mortgage redemption payments.

COST CALCULATOR: MOVING				
House price	£50,000	£100,000	£250,000	£500,000
Legal	£300	£450	£600	£700
Estate agency fees[1]	£900	£1800	£4500	£9000
Moving fees	£500	£750	£1000	£2000
VAT element (at 17.5%)	£297	£525	£1067	£1700
Total cost	£1997	£3525	£7167	£13,400

[1] Based on an average commission fee of 1.8%

THE VALUE OF YOUR HOME

Property values are frequently headline news, and people often contemplate the value of their property versus what they paid for it. Needless to say, everybody wants to have made money on their house – it means that, when they come to move, the next property can be larger and/or more desirable, or the mortgage can be that little bit smaller.

While property does (generally) go up in value, realistically your property is only worth what someone is willing to pay for it at the time it is advertised for sale. For this reason, it's worth doing a bit of research before calling in the estate agents. In that way, you can gauge what the market is like, what kind of properties are up for sale and, most importantly, what kind of prices different properties are achieving.

To start your research, look at some local property papers. Usually you find these in an estate agent's office or they are pushed through your door once a week. Local newspapers – either bought or delivered free – also often have a property section. Study these papers for a few weeks to see what's on offer.

Once you have the background materials, sit down with a large tea, coffee (or more convivial beverage) and a pen and paper and start thinking about your own property. What are its main features and selling points compared with the properties for sale? To compare more easily, make a table listing all the important points, with your property at the top and add other similar properties for sale (see overleaf).

QUICK TIP **Use web property portals, too, if you like (see page 83). But beware: these may not be as up-to-date as local newspapers or the windows of estate agents.**

EASY VALUE COMPARISON (see bottom of page 13 and below)								
	Number of		Garden	Garage	Property age	Type of property[1]	Type of area[2]	Price	Estate agent
	Bedrooms	Bathrooms							
My property	3	2	Yes	No	1930s	Detached	Rural	£100k	Name
Property 1									
Property 2									
Property 3									

[1] e.g. detached, terraced
[2] e.g. suburban, estate

Be objective – memories and love for your home may be strong, but unfortunately don't make it worth more. Imagine yourself as the buyer – not the seller.

Once you've filled in the table, it will be easier to think like a buyer.

Now, start asking yourself some questions. Are there a lot of properties like yours on the market — or only a few? Over several weeks, is your type of property selling quickly or slowly?

Make sure you remain detached when doing your comparison. Check the list with your partner, family or friends to make sure you continue to be objective and are not letting those memories colour your conclusions. Now that you have a good idea of what estate agents call 'comparables', check to see over the next few weeks which estate agents are selling properties similar to yours. It's also a good idea to have a quick look around the neighbourhood to see which properties are up for sale (and with which agents) as not all properties will be advertised in the papers. Do your own market watch over the next few weeks, checking on which agents are really selling properties compared with the ones who just have 'For Sale' signs up.

Armed with this well-thought-through buyers' view of the market, you should now:

- Have a good idea of the minimum and maximum value of your home
- Know which estate agents are most likely to have buyers with properties similar to yours and are achieving sales.

Now the exciting bit begins. Get some estate agents in to value your home. And don't believe everything you hear about estate agents. They are not all out to get you.

THE VALUE OF AN
ESTATE AGENT

Rarely have I seen a good word about estate agents in the press. Dinner party conversation tends to vilify rather than praise. But – believe me – good estate agents exist and are probably more common than you think.

Because people tend to go for the estate agent that offers the lowest cost or the highest value on a property, the best agent is not always the one chosen. Agents that charge the least amount often do so because they offer a service to match. Other agents recommend a high price to encourage you to take their business, sometimes knowing that they will have to persuade you at some stage to reduce your price to the one that other agents originally suggested.

So what do estate agents do? Actually, quite a lot.

When selling a property, estate agents are working for you, the vendor. Their main aim should be to sell your property as quickly and efficiently as possible – and at the highest price achievable. This value is based on the number of buyers looking for a property like yours. So estate agents need to know of people looking for a property of a similar type and  price in your area. They find these buyers by advertising (usually for a fee) on the web, in local newspapers and magazines, and by using 'For Sale' or 'Sold' boards. Of course, window displays in their offices are another way of attracting buyers. Once somebody is interested, an estate agent provides details of the property (see page 16).

As soon as the estate agent has some interest, he needs to make sure the person is serious about buying your property and not just having a look around. Estate agents should always ask buyers what their circumstances are:

- Do they have a property to sell?
- Are they cash buyers?
- Do they have the funds approved to purchase?
- If their property is under offer, how robust is the potential sale?
- Have surveys and legal details been done or not even started?

A good agent will only introduce serious buyers to your property.

If you want to avoid a lot of people visiting – and not taking it any further – you may want to stipulate that only people who are 'under offer' or are cash buyers are invited to view the property. The downside to this approach is that someone who may want to buy your property won't get to see it. Remember: fewer people looking at the property may translate into a longer wait for an offer.

NUMBER CRUNCHING

- 85% of people sell their homes through estate agents

- 8% through auctions

- 7% sell privately

THE TRUTH AND NOTHING BUT THE TRUTH

Agents are legally bound by the Estate Agency Act and the Property Misdescriptions Act to give accurate details of a property or they can be prosecuted. In order to produce this information they will need to:

- Visit your property
- Measure each room
- Write up information in detail
- Take photos (inside and out)

Using new technologies they may also produce floor plans and 360-degree virtual 'walk-throughs'. For large properties, brochures are often produced, which can sometimes be downloaded from the Internet in the form of a PDF (portable document format). But, at this level of sale you often have to pay for the privilege. Some agents do these extras themselves, while others call in specialist companies.

COMPARING AGENTS

A good way to decide if an estate agent produces good sales material is to compare the property details produced by a selection of agents. Put yourself in the position of a buyer, and see which ones you think are best. Basic room measurements are one thing, but what about information on the location or local amenities? Do the details inspire you and make you want to see the property?

Once the details on your property are produced, the agent's job is to advertise your property by contacting potential buyers, usually by telephone, email, the post, advertisements or handouts. Some agents are also able to send SMS messages to your mobile phone, giving potential buyers an edge on viewing properties coming onto the market.

Remember that you are trying to find the best agents to sell your home. The more you know about them and their methods, hopefully the better they will manage your sale.

If the agent is doing his job correctly, then all this advertising activity will lead to viewings. Usually, you will find that the more viewings, the better the agent. Equally, if your property is at the right price and in the right location, good agents are able to ensure that a high percentage of people looking at your home either ask for a second viewing or make an offer on the property.

Agents have different views on their involvement after you accept an offer. Some think it's their responsibility to help liaise with the buyer, solicitors or conveyancers (see page 123), surveyor and even the companies arranging the finance. Some agents even go so far as to have specialist sales progression people or departments to help track your move at every stage, ensuring it progresses efficiently to completion (when you hand the keys over to the buyer).

Other agents believe their job ends at the offer and let you sort out all the rest – unless, of course, if the sale falls through and the entire process begins all over again.

So, are agents value for (your) money? The answer is – generally. It is always in the interest of your estate agent to sell your property quickly and efficiently. Remember, they do everything for free and are only paid when your property sale is completed.

On average, an estate agent spends approximately £500 selling a property before they earn any money.

HOW TO PICK A GOOD AGENT

Most people think estate agents are all the same. They aren't. Like almost everything else in life, they come in all shapes and sizes. There are specific types of agents, some who get a low wage, which is topped up by commission monies received for the number of properties they sell.

EASY ESTATE AGENT GUIDE

Estate agents come in a variety of flavours. Here is a list of the main ones.

Corporates are agents with national coverage, usually with financial, legal and surveying services also available.
Examples: Your Move, Halifax, Bairstow Eves (Countrywide).

Large independents have wide local coverage and either their own services or links with other companies.
Examples: Townends, Hamptons, Keith Pattinson.

Local independents are typically owned by a local person who has been around for a long time and who has often set up their own estate agency or a surveyor who has expanded into estate agency.

Tied agents are usually smaller estate agencies that are 'tied' to a financial institution.
Example: Legal and General has over 1400 tied agents.

Others get a better salary with less commission. Some companies feel too high a commission-led salary can lead to agents not working in the interest of the client.

Your initial research (see page 17) should give you an idea of the local agents that are good at selling your type of property. By doing this research, you should also have an idea of the maximum/minimum sale price of your property.

The next step is to contact your selected agents (by telephone or email) to make sure they cover your area. Remember that different agents cover different postcodes and specific areas no matter where their office is. It is also worth checking (particularly with national agents) that they advertise in the local papers in your area.

When contacting agents, note how quickly they answer you. Little things are important. For example, does someone always answer the phone and if not can you leave a message? If they offer to ring back, do they do it within a reasonable time? Are they polite and helpful? You are about to trust them with the biggest sale of your life. They need to be as keen for the sale as you are.

KEEPING ESTATE AGENTS
IN LINE

Although estate agents are not officially regulated, they often ascribe to codes of practice set by associations. These bodies are excellent indicators of good service, so it's worth checking whether your prospective agents are members.

National Association of Estate Agents (NAEA)

The NAEA is a trade body that members pay to join. It has its own code of practice and offers an independent help line for the public (see Making contact, opposite).

Individuals, not companies, are members. You often see the logo advertised in their offices and on their literature.

For the general public, the main benefit of an NAEA affiliated estate agent is that members take their obligations and work seriously. The NAEA itself is a trade body and as such its members have access to extensive research on the home buying and selling process, and training is provided for themselves and their staff. All of this should mean they are able to offer a better standard of service to you. It also acts as an 'industry voice', and as a result you often see them quoted by the media.

Royal Institute of Chartered Surveyors (RICS)

Some estate agencies begin life as survey providers. The companies start by assessing properties but then expand into a full estate agency service as this increases turnover and attracts further survey work. As a result, some estate agency practices will have a RICS affiliation instead of, or as well as, the NAEA, or they'll be signed up to the Ombudsman Scheme.

If an agent does not belong to the scheme or the organisations above, it does not automatically mean they are no good. However, it does help you to differentiate between agents. Always ask what memberships or associations your agency has, as some may also be members of local initiatives or schemes that show their commitment to honest and fair business dealing with buyers and sellers.

MAKING CONTACT

National Association of Estate Agents (NAEA)
Tel: **01926 496800**
Website: **www.naea.co.uk**

Royal Institute of Chartered Surveyors (RICS)
Tel: **0870 333 1600**
Website: **www.ricsfirms.co.uk**

Ombudsman scheme
Tel: **01727 333306**
Website: **www.oea.co.uk**

Ombudsman scheme

This is a private and voluntary scheme established to give dissatisfied house buyers and sellers access to an independent complaints review procedure.

The Ombudsman provides a process under which an independent body addresses disputes between member agents and their clients (you). It is open to all estate agents, such as members of the National Association of Estate Agents (NAEA) and Royal Institute of Chartered Surveyors (RICS).

All agents who belong sign a code of practice, which lays out a procedure to follow if any disputes arise (it covers you both as buyer and seller).

Basically the code is a way to sort the good from the bad, encouraging agents to provide the highest level of service. Agents who join must also hold insurance to cover any claims. So unless an agent is running a successful business, it is difficult for them to fund the premium.

INTERVIEWING THE AGENT

Once you have screened your list of agents, invite the successful ones to view your property. Let them look around first and then sit down together and ask them to talk about how their estate agency operates, its values, work methods and success stories (similar properties they have sold). Don't be afraid to ask lots of questions (see opposite). This is your big chance to get to know the agents and make sure they are people in whom you feel confident.

DON'T GET LOCKED IN

Some agents are rather unscrupulous at getting your business and then locking you into a long-term contract. The two tactics most often used are suggesting a very high selling price and offering a very low commission or fee. Although both (and especially combined) can be tempting, it is important that you ask several other questions of agents before you trust them with the sale of probably your largest asset. The following section helps to explain how to pick a good estate agent and what type of questions to ask and then how to agree what terms you both work to.

When you have answers for all of the above questions, it is the time to talk to the agents about what they think your property is worth. You will also have your own idea from your research as to what you expect them to say.

QUESTIONS FOR YOUR AGENT

- How long have you been in business?
- How many instructions (sales) have you had and how many completed sales from these have you made in the past three months and six months?
- How many buyers do you have on your books?
- Where do you advertise – property websites, newspapers, magazines, your office windows, local billboards, 'For Sale' signs?
- Do you make floor plans or take photos yourself or does someone else do them?
- How do you use technology to help your sales? (For example, do they SMS, email, have any tracking systems for the number of viewers, second viewings?)
- How many people do you intend to contact and send my property details to?
- Who will be showing people around my property?
- How often will you give me feedback on my property viewings and how will you give me this information?
- Is there anything you recommend I should do to the property to help you sell it?
- Once an offer is made, how are you able to help speed progress to completion?

If the agents you have interviewed are within the price range you expected, then your choice should be determined by who you feel most confident in – the agent who you think will help sell your home quickly and painlessly. If there are agents that come in much higher or much lower – and they cannot really justify their prices with comparable properties – then you are better going with the agent that offers the mid-price and/or is closest to your own research.

GETTING A VALUATION

Estate agents look at the actual selling price of properties, as well as the typical advertised price. When there are more buyers than sellers and the market is going up, the actual sale may be around the asking price or slightly higher. But when the market is falling – there are more sellers than buyers – the sale price is often less than what was advertised.

When agents offer a valuation they ask what you think the property is worth or what you are hoping to sell it for. This is why it is a good idea to have researched the market – you should already have a feel for the

QUICK TIP **Ask your estate agent(s) for a 'quick sale' and a 'wait and see' price. This should give you an idea of how much they understand the market.**

selling price and will have some realistic expectations. When the agent quotes you a figure, get him or her to back it up with recent sales of other comparable properties. The agent's valuation should be based on:

- The popularity and desirability of the area and road
- Internal and external property décor and condition
- Surrounding buildings and neighbours
- Whether you have additional features, such as a conservatory, extensions and/or conversions
- Off-street parking, garage or guaranteed parking space

This list is not exhaustive. Many other things play a part in pricing a property, including whether your home is near good transport links (trains and motorways, for example), general amenities (shopping centres) and schools. Other more intangible and subjective elements also play a part. These include things like fashionable décor – for example decking – and the modernity of key rooms such as the bathroom and kitchen.

Once an agent has talked with you about your reasons for moving (remember, they do not get paid until they sell your home, so they need to make sure you are serious about the change) and looked around your property, they will then recommend two things: a selling price (the price at which they recommend you market the property) and a price to accept (this may be lower than the price at which they market the property).

After the visit, every agent should confirm in writing any suggestions they made and give you the details of how they are describing your property in the form of a brochure or leaflet. They should also give you a contract detailing terms and conditions.

QUICK TIP

Don't lock yourself into too long a period of sole agency. Most agents try for a minimum of 12 weeks, sometimes more. I recommend no more than six to eight weeks.

AGREEING THE DEAL

So now you've had the beauty pageant and you're ready to choose the winner – or winners. But once you choose your estate agent(s) the work doesn't stop. Many people become disillusioned with their agent quite quickly. You can avoid this by not only being careful in your choice, but working with – not against – your agent to sell the property.

Some handy hints of how to do this are:

- Ensure you agree how soon property details will be completed and if these will include floor plans and photos.
- Agree which papers and magazines the property will be advertised in and how often.
- Find out if your property will be featured (until sold) in the agent's window.
- Have you agreed to have a 'For Sale' board?
- Make sure you are clear about when you prefer people to view your home and how much notice the agent will give you. Also agree exactly who is responsible for showing likely buyers around – you or the agent.
- Do you have a preference as to which estate agent employee shows your property?
- Check where your house will come on the list for potential buyers – will it be at the beginning of a long list of viewings or at the end?
- Agree how often and how much feedback you receive from viewings.
- Be clear about just how long you are willing to wait for a sale.
- If you can, get the agent to agree a minimum/maximum number of viewings for the first four weeks. Not everyone will be happy about this, but confident (and competent) estate agents shouldn't have a problem with it. Make sure you get the agreement in writing, too.
- Agree in writing what will happen after offer stage (see page 49).

SOLE OR MULTIPLE AGREEMENT?

No matter who you chose, all agents need you to sign an agreement with them. This is partly so they can legally gain their fee once your home is sold. However, the agreement also ensures that you cannot simply sell your home privately, having been introduced to the buyer by the agent.

A sole agency agreement is where you give your business to only one estate agent. You agree this on a set time basis and for an agreed commission or fee. Typically, this will cost less than a multiple agency because the agent has no competitors. **A multiple agency agreement** is where you give your business to more than one agent, usually two (as you can't legally put up more than two 'For Sale' boards on any one property). However, there is nothing to stop you having more agents if you don't use boards. This type of agreement usually costs more, as the agents are competing against each other to sell your property with only one able to claim the money at the end.

Which should you choose? It's really up to you. The **benefit** of a multiple agency agreement is that you have at least two agents trying to sell your property – with both distributing your details to their prospective buyer lists, a sale is more likely to happen quickly. Also, if your property falls on the fringes of two distinct areas, it may be beneficial to have two agents who cover slightly different locations, because in that way the catchment area of potential buyers is greater. Of course, the **downside** is that whichever agent gets the sale, you will pay a greater commission than you would have on a single agency agreement.

The last, and possibly the most important, point to agree is the fee – whether it will be commission-based or fixed. Most agents settle for a commission. They will also offer this based on sole or multiple agencies (see above). What you negotiate is really up to you. For example, you can try offering a higher commission the closer they get to your asking price.

Sometimes if other agents are offering less, say 1–1.5% compared with 2%, you can get a deal where the lower fee applies up to a certain price. You can also agree that if the asking price is met or the house is sold within a specified time limit that's important to you, they get the full 2%.

One option is to negotiate first with a sole agent, setting a specific time frame (say four to six weeks) to sell your home. If they haven't sold in that time, you can then ask another agent to step in and move to a multiple agency agreement. You may be able to negotiate retaining the original sole agency commission and may get the second agent to agree to a sole agency rate too. Alternatively, you may have to agree to move to the higher commission structure for a multiple agreement.

SELLING IT **YOURSELF**

You may, however, decide you want to sell your property yourself. If you are confident and have the time to invest in what's needed to sell your property, it may indeed be the right thing to do.

If you want to do this, you need to understand what you can and cannot say or write about a property. This is detailed by the Property Misdescriptions Act. It's also worth knowing that when selling the property yourself there are companies that can help you. You have to pay up front for this — the costs are around £30 to £100 — but it costs a lot less than an estate agent. Some of these companies provide you with your own 'For Sale' board and/or space on their website to advertise your property. They can also advertise the website to help increase your access to potential buyers. You do not have to produce details for these companies, but if you do, make sure they are legally accurate.

CHECK OUT YOUR LEAD

When talking to people on the phone, try to establish whether they really are serious buyers. Key questions should be:

- Are you a cash buyer?
- Do you have a property for sale? If so, is it under offer? And when would you ideally like to move?

It also helps to understand why potential buyers are moving. This gives you time to think through how your property and its location may be suitable to them.

If you start attracting viewers, make sure you have their contact details (telephone, mobile, address, email, for example). Not only will this indicate how serious they are as potential buyers, it also helps to deter unscrupulous people whose interests really lie in viewing your possessions

QUICK TIP Typically 80% of people buy a home near where they already live. Boards are a good way to advertise your sale, but are less common in rural areas – the worry is that if you're too remote, burglars will be stopping by, not prospective buyers.

If your property isn't what the viewer is seeking, try to find out why. Did your property not fulfil a specific requirement, or did it not match the viewers' expectations? Is the problem something you can fix (like the price) or is it something you can't change (the road where you live)?

WHAT TO DO NEXT

If you are fortunate enough to receive an offer, the procedure for accepting and seeing the sale through to completion is pretty much the same as when selling through an agent (see page 44). However, because you will be doing all the work the estate agent normally does, you will need to verify that the buyer can afford the property. To do this, ring the buyer's agent and check that any property they are selling is under offer or sold. Alternatively, you could ask the buyer for some evidence that their property is under offer – a letter from their solicitor, for example. Find out if a survey has yet to be carried out on their property – this will help to give you some idea of how far down the process your buyer is.

You will also need to gain a mortgage agreement in principle (see page 77). Alternatively, ask for a letter from the buyer's bank or independent financial advisor to confirm that your buyer has a mortgage agreement or the funds to go through with the purchase. It's worth the effort: one in three sales fall through after the offer stage mainly because of poor finances. It's also a good idea to compose a letter confirming your buyer's address and solicitor's details, as well as details of your legal representation and the agreed price. Send this letter to your buyer and legal representative – it should help kick-start the legal process (see page 44).

PREPARING YOUR HOME
FOR SALE

A few years ago the idea of preparing your home for sale was a very unfamiliar concept. You would simply put your home on the market and hope. Granted, when the property market is rising, houses are easier to sell. Buyers know they have to act quickly or face the possibility of losing their 'dream home'. However, in a slower market, preparation is essential. Buyers have many more homes to choose from, so if you spend the time making yours stand out, the more likely you are to clinch that sale.

Today's buyers want to get the most they can for their money: the most space, function and potential. Also, today's buyers tend to be very busy people, preferring to use what leisure time they have for recreation. Most of them are looking for a home (if paying top-dollar) that they can move into immediately and not have to spend a lot of time or money on. Whether the market is slow or fast, keeping one step ahead of the buyers is key to ensuring that as a seller you get your price (or higher) and secure that sale. The best way of doing this is by presenting your home to appeal to the broadest buying audience both inside and out. Where do you begin?

THE PSYCHOLOGY OF HOME BUYING

There has been a good deal of research into **what people want from a home**, which reinforces what I have been preaching for years. In her article titled 'The Psychology of Home Buying', Dr Louise Payne, Clinical Psychologist at St Mary's Hospital, states the following: 'People tend to look for a place that they feel **is in keeping with their personality**, or in keeping with how they wish to be perceived. … Because people tend to look at homes as a medium through which to say something about themselves, it is important that psychologically they are able to imagine themselves as **being at home in the property they are viewing**. … Many people are unable to look beyond the initial presentation … and imagine how it could be transformed with clever colour schemes and so on.'

KERB APPEAL

Begin outdoors. Stand across the road from your home and assess how your home compares with the others in your neighbourhood. How does it measure up? Does it grab your attention? A prospective buyer is most likely to drive by your house first to see if he's interested and will only bother to go inside if he likes what he sees. This is what is known as kerb appeal and is extremely important. If a buyer is not impressed at the kerb, you've lost a potential sale before you've had half a chance.

Your house should be appealing and welcoming, one of the nicest on the street, yet in keeping with the style of its surroundings. Fresh paintwork, a well-manicured garden and the overall first impression of a cared-for home are important ingredients for enticing buyers inside.

AMBIENCE

You may not know this, but it has been proven that buyers make the decision whether or not to buy within the first 60–90 seconds of having entered a house. But how is this possible if they haven't yet even seen the house? Well, the fact of the matter is that the buyer himself may not even be aware of his decision because it has been made subconsciously. Although most buyers have a list of requirements for their next purchase, the decision whether to buy a certain house or not is usually made based on intangibles. It has to 'feel' right. And if it doesn't, they are out the door as fast they came in.

TOP TEN TIPS FOR CREATING KERB APPEAL

1   **Repair anything that needs fixing,** such as broken or cracked pavements or walkways, fences or gates, doorbells and windows. Repaint or touch up where necessary.

2   **Pay close attention to windows.** They must be super clean and free of clutter on the sills. Check that all window coverings look as tidy from the outside as they do from the inside.

3   **Notice what is parked in front of the house.** Be sure that there are no unsightly cars, skips, etc. If they belong to your nearest neighbours, try to speak to them about relocating them for the time your house is for sale.

4   **Remove all unnecessary items** from in front of the house such as rubbish bins, bicycles and children's toys. Be sure there is a clear, defined path to the front door.

5   **Check outdoor lighting** making sure it is operative and adequate for viewing.

6   **Be sure you have house numbers** that can be seen from the street. How can a buyer view your house if he can't find it?

7   **Pay close attention to the front door.** A lick of paint in a distinctive colour always helps (I prefer a rich red). Polish or replace all door furniture, fix the locks and make sure the door does not stick when opened.

8   **Be sure your garden is in top form.** Trim all overgrown trees or shrubs, mow the lawn and sweep and clean everything. Invest in some flowering seasonal plants and/or shrubs to give the front of your house more appeal.

9   **Place a new doormat in front of the front door.** I like to use a 'Welcome' mat as it gives a positive subliminal message to a buyer.

10 **Be sure that your 'For Sale' sign is clearly visible.** You don't want any missed opportunities.

So what can you do to make your house 'feel' right? First, you need to pay close attention to those hidden subliminal suggestions, a technique that is used often in advertising. Good lighting is essential, both natural and ambient, creating a cheerful atmosphere, and colours should be soft, neutral and easy on the eye. Cleanliness and order throughout evoke a 'looked after' feeling in the home. Soft background music puts the buyer at ease. Subtle fresh scents as well as plants and flowers add life and vitality to a room. A fire in the fireplace on a chilly day creates the feeling of homeliness, as does the old trick of something yummy baking in the oven. And pets, children and sellers themselves should remain unobtrusive in order to let the prospective buyers view the home in a relaxed and comfortable manner.

SPACE

A buyer has to be able to imagine himself and his things living in your house and it is your job to make this as easy as possible to visualise. Since space is always at a premium, you need to make the most of what you have at hand. Edit your belongings ruthlessly and arrange furniture to allow freedom of movement. Now, more than ever, 'less is more' (money in your pocket, that is). Remember, if a buyer cannot see a room, he is not going to mentally move in. Clear out all closets and cupboards, and put everything back in a neat, organised manner. A buyer needs to feel that there is adequate room for all his belongings, not get the impression that even you are struggling for storage. Take advantage of unused storage space in the house – lofts, basements, garages, under stairs, etc. – and neatly present it as an asset, not an eyesore. Never, ever, present one of your bedrooms (no matter how small) as a box room. You are leaving money on the table.

Pay special attention to your kitchen and bathroom(s). As these are two areas that can be the most costly to redo, buyers tend to scrutinise these areas carefully. Few buyers have the money left over after purchasing their new home to do any major remodelling, so they need to feel that the kitchen and bathrooms are in 'move-in', and useable, condition. Sometimes it takes as little as a lick of paint on walls or cabinets, new flooring and/or tiling and some updated lighting to make a kitchen or bathroom look and feel new.

When preparing your home to sell, it is critical to know where to spend your money in order to realise your greatest return. You want to put your time, money and effort where it counts. The following section is a guide to spending less than £500 on each room and getting the most out of your cash.

Entrance hall

- The colours used here should be a preview of the colour scheme for the rest of the house. If your paintwork needs refreshing, don't hesitate to redecorate. Choose a warm neutral colour for the walls. You want the buyer to feel 'welcome' immediately upon entering.
- Have a place for everything – coats, umbrellas, post, etc. – to avoid clutter. Keep all clutter well organised and behind closed doors. Build in shelving, hanging rails, shoe racks or boxes in existing cupboards, or in wasted spaces, such as underneath the stairs.
- Good lighting is critical. If necessary, add a new ceiling fixture or wall sconces. These can be decorative elements as well as serving a practical purpose.
- Replace worn carpet in the hallway or on the stairs with a medium-coloured neutral, hardwearing carpet. Or if you have floorboards, refinish them if necessary and add an area rug or runner to complement your scheme and décor.
- If an unattractive radiator is prominent, consider a decorative cover, making it into a feature rather than an eyesore.
- A mirror is a must. It adds interest, reflects light, and acts as a final checkpoint on the way out the door. There are many styles and sizes available to complement your overall scheme.
- Fresh flowers and/or plants are always a cheerful and welcoming sight and add a touch of life. They cost very little and brighten up even the dullest of spaces.
- If space permits, create a seating area. A settee or bench can look lovely as well as be a practical place to sit and wait for friends or taxis.

Since the entrance of your home is the first statement you make to the public, it is extremely important yet often neglected and used simply as a 'pass through' area or dumping ground. Think about how you want to present yourself and your family to the world.

Living room

- Neutralise your overall colour scheme. Redecorate walls and woodwork if shabby or inappropriate.
- Create ambience with lighting. Add lamps or spots if necessary. Have all major lights on controllable dimmers.
- Replace worn or tatty carpets. Refinish floorboards and purchase an attractive rug for both visual and actual warmth.
- A focal point is essential. If one doesn't already exist architecturally, then create one. Add a mantle, highlight an antique or special piece of furniture, or create an interesting arrangement on a console table using a favourite collection or grouping of objects.

This room sets the tone for the rest of the house – the lifestyle you hope to create for the buyer. For this reason it is one of the most important rooms when selling.

- Purchase or build an entertainment centre to house all your electronic equipment including the television if possible. Or customise one out of a refurbished flea market armoire.
- If upholstered furniture is worn or soiled, have it steam cleaned or cover with a throw or slipcover.
- If furniture is beyond repair or outdated, consider purchasing or hiring a few key pieces. Make sure they are suitably scaled to the size of your room and arranged to allow for easy traffic flow.
- Change your window coverings. Blinds maximise space and add a more modern feel. Curtains should co-ordinate with the overall colour scheme in the room.
- Invest in some colourful accents such as throws, cushions or interesting objects to help tie the room together. Remember that these can go with you when you move.
- Space permitting, create cosy vignettes such as window seats, reading nooks or a games table … be aspirational.
- Invest in some prints or original artwork that is uplifting and enhances your colour scheme. Alternatively, you can make your own with paints and canvas.

Dining room

- Refinish your dining table or cover with a nice cloth or table runner.
- Slipcover your dining chairs or re-upholster the chair seat covers.
- For added ambience, install a chandelier in the ceiling above the centre of the dining table.
- Have a centrepiece on your table that creates a focal point. This can be a plant, a vase of flowers, a beautiful bowl, a candle arrangement … anything that will focus the eye on the centre of the room.
- Thin out and dress sideboards and Welsh dressers with your finest crockery or crystal. Consider adding shelves for displaying these items if you lack space.
- Accessorise with themed artwork, candles, fresh table linens.
- If your dining room must serve a dual purpose, such as home office, build it into a corner where it can be hidden from view when necessary. If it won't fit into a piece of furniture, buy or make a folding screen to put in front.

Often this is the most neglected room in the house because it is not used on a regular basis. Nevertheless, buyers want to know that they can have a sit-down dinner party if they so choose. It is your job as a seller to make it perfectly clear.

Kitchen

The proverbial 'heart of the home', when selling, the condition of your kitchen can make or break a sale. Often an inexpensive cosmetic face-lift can make it appear nearly new.

- Replace worn flooring.
- Replace or repair counter tops or splashbacks.
- Paint, reface or replace cupboard doors.
- Install new door hardware for a more modern look.
- Replace or paint broken or chipped tiles and clean grout.
- Box in unsightly exposed pipes and boilers and paint them the colour of the walls to blend in.
- If necessary, replace taps, sink, cooker and hob with something more modern.
- Create an eating space for at lease two persons by adding a table and chairs or breakfast bar and stools.
- Add additional lighting, especially above the cupboards and over the workspace.
- Accessorise using co-ordinated crockery, appliances, tea towels and place mats.
- Install a new blind.

Bedroom

- Banish all extraneous items from the bedroom such as televisions, computers and fax machines. Or if this is not possible, hide them behind closed doors.
- Clear out cupboards and install hanging racks, shelving and organisers or containers for loose items.
- Consider installing fitted bedroom furniture if space is at a premium.
- Buy new bedding and accessories.
- Buy new blinds or curtains to co-ordinate with the bedding.
- If you have the space, create a sitting area. It will make the room feel more like a luxurious suite.
- Accessorise with serene prints, fresh flowers, candles and a FEW of your favourite personal objects.
- If you have a box room or 'nothing' room, turn it into something such as a guest room, playroom, home office or combination.

The number, size and condition of bedrooms in a home can greatly affect your sale price.

Bathroom

- If your suite is an outdated colour, replace it with an inexpensive white one or have it refaced by a professional.
- Replace the flooring.
- Upgrade the lighting. Install wall sconces or make-up lights.

If your bathroom is not new, then it has to at least look new.

- Build in a medicine cabinet, vanity unit or additional storage.
- Add a power shower and an extractor fan.
- Install new taps.
- Clean, repaint or replace tiles and grout.
- Buy a new decorative mirror, or mirror an entire wall if the bathroom is undersized or dark.
- Purchase a new toilet seat.
- Buy a new shower curtain.
- Buy new fluffy towels and a bath mat.
- Accessorise with pretty glass bottles, scented soaps and candles, and a plant or two.

Garden

The garden when utilised can act as an additional room in your house. Don't ignore it, no matter what the season.

- Clear out and trim all bushes and overgrowth.
- Define property boundaries with plantings or fencing.
- Repair, rebuild or install a new fence.
- Install new turf or patio surface.
- Replant your garden with seasonal flowering plants.
- Install sprinklers or drip irrigation.
- Install outdoor lighting.
- Buy a shed for items that are frequently used.
- Invest in some attractive outdoor furniture.

LEGALLY LETTING GO

Understanding the conveyancing process is the key to understanding how to buy and sell a home. This section explains the legal process of selling a home in detail and gives timeframes for each step, so you know what to expect and when.

MAKING SENSE OF CONVEYANCING

Conveyancing is a term you will hear often. Most people find it confusing but it needn't be. Basically, it's a specialist term used to describe the paperwork needed to transfer the ownership of a property from one person to another. You are legally allowed to do this yourself, but most people prefer to let professionals handle the process. Choosing who does your legal work is as important as choosing your estate agent. A good conveyancer or solicitor can make the difference between a good or a bad selling experience and sometimes even whether the sale goes ahead.

CHOOSING THE RIGHT LEGAL PERSON

Any trained solicitor can practise conveyancing. However, if they do not specialise in this area, you might be better off finding one who does. Or you may already use a legal practice that has a specialist department or person covering conveyancing. If not, talk to friends and neighbours who have recently moved and ask them for a recommendation.

 If you live in England and Wales, you also have the option of using a licensed conveyancer. Although these are not fully-fledged solicitors, they are sanctioned by the Council of Licensed Conveyancers and specialise in property transactions. When receiving quotes from firms, make sure they list everything you need to pay and not just their own fee. For example, ensure they include local search fees, mortgage valuation costs, office copy entry costs (see page 46). You should compare like with like.

QUICK TIP

If you already have a good conveyancer or a legal firm and are happy with their work, stick with them. But if you do, make sure they have a specialist knowledge in conveyancing. It won't hurt to also check their rates compared with others companies who are on-line as you may be able to negotiate a discount.

In the past, most conveyancing was done by a local practice, heavily paper dependent and terribly slow. Many people complained at having to chase their solicitor. On top of this, few people, if any, really understood what was happening on a daily basis.

CONVEYANCING IMPROVEMENTS

Conveyancing has changed dramatically over the years. With the realisation that the time for offer, exchange and completion can be very long, the industry, along with the government, is trying to improve the process.

At the same time, companies are offering consumers a better deal to attract more business. In all honesty, there is a natural conflict between the conveyancing work that needs to be done and the seller's need to be constantly updated on what is happening. Most people doing conveyancing work have to concentrate on detailed paperwork, co-ordinate contact between the mortgage lender, government departments, you and the other legal parties while at the same time keeping the agents in the loop. By the time contracts are exchanged or completed (see page 45) the conveyancer is usually concentrating on several things at once, all falling at the end of a month, while trying to field the constant phone calls from the various parties all anxious to know what's happening. The result is often frustration (and sometimes anger) all around, further adding to everyone's stress levels.

More annoyingly, most local practices typically work a nine-to-five day, making it even harder for buyers and sellers to make contact at a time convenient to them, which can be outside a busy working day.

Many companies recognise these issues and are addressing the problems, particularly of communication. Some companies now operate call centres, specifically designed to field your questions. Many are open in the evenings, some at weekends.

Some companies are now also using the Internet to allow on-line tracking of the process. These systems explain each stage of the process – and some of them can now inform you by email or SMS alerts when key steps are completed. These innovations benefit you by making the process less of a mystery and allowing you involvement and assurance of progress

QUICK TIP **Make sure when you consider taking out your next mortgage to check how efficient the lender is at drawing down deeds or you may have problems the next time you move.**

Such innovations as emails and SMS alerts help you to keep track of the process, showing you where (and what) the hold-ups are, and generally keep you out of the hair of the conveyancer so he or she can get on with it.

without slowing the process by interrupting the work. To gain competitive edge, some companies also offer a 'no sale, no fee' service. This is a really good idea. Even if the sale falls through (for example, if a survey detects a problem or issue), you may still have to pay for some things – like local search fees – but at least you won't have to pay for the solicitor's time. Fixed fee services mean you can budget more easily.

WHO, WHAT AND WHEN

Every sale and purchase is different, particularly in Britain where much of the property information can go back decades, if not centuries.

The legal aspects of selling a property are much less involved than for buying, so costs are often lower. Many people think if they are selling they have to wait for an offer before starting the legal side. But this is not the case. If you are definitely selling, you can instruct a conveyancer the same day you put your property on the market, or any day after that. This enables important title deeds to be applied for and contracts drawn up. It can especially help if the property being sold is leasehold as third parties will need to be contacted by the legal company.

One good reason to instruct early is that it shows your agent and buyers you are serious about moving. If you get a buyer who is keen to move quickly, a lot of the work on your side is already done. This can knock weeks off the process. With no sale, no fee conveyancing you can also reduce the risk of losing money if something does go wrong. But make sure you check the costs of pulling out before you commit yourself.

HOW LONG SHOULD THIS PROCESS LAST?

The faster the paperwork – and the more efficient those dealing with it – the faster the process. Bottlenecks occur because you have not completed

MAKING CONTACT

Online conveyancing:
Website: **www.easier2move.co.uk**
Tel: **07004 327437**

Legal advice and conveyancing:
Website: **www.fidler.co.uk**
Tel: **01623 451111**

paperwork correctly, lenders or government departments are slow to respond or send information, or the buyer's solicitor is playing for time and asking lots of questions.

Ideally, to get from offer to exchange should be possible in only four weeks. From exchange to completion in two weeks. So the entire process could be only six weeks. If only. How do you achieve this much-sought-for goal? Well, do as much work up front with your legal company as you can. Provide them with your 'mortgage reference' or 'roll' number as soon as you instruct them so they can draw down the deeds or gain the office copy entries early. This will speed up the sale further down the road. If you can get a draft contract to your buyer relatively quickly, they are less likely to drag their heels and completion could soon follow. When you are heading towards exchange, double check that your buyer has their deposit ready either via your estate agent or your legal company. Finally, answer or return any queries or papers sent to you by your legal company without delay. There are reports of the process taking just one day. Yes, this is possible, but highly unusual. And only likely if most of the work needed is done well before.

But no matter how efficient you are, the negotiations can drag on. I know of one case where the buyer's solicitor was causing problems over an extension that had been built years ago and questioned whether planning permission was required. The solution was for the purchaser to gain an insurance policy (organised by the buyer's solicitor at a few hundred pounds) in case this ever became an issue. Most legal companies are efficient. Others can be a real pain, making sure every 'i' is dotted, every 't' crossed. Remember – the final decision rests with you and the buyer. But some legal eagles like to drag things out, possibly in the hope of higher fees – yet another reason to favour fixed fee conveyancing.

TEN LEGAL STEPS
TO SELLING YOUR HOME

The following steps explain the key stages to legally transferring ownership of your home to another person. It is important you keep track of what has or has not been done as each of these steps progresses your sale towards exchange and then completion. Unless you are doing the conveyancing yourself, all of these steps and the forms should be initiated/sent by your conveyancer. If they are not at any stage, then you should contact your conveyancing company and ask them when each of these steps is going to happen. Once you have filled in any forms or signed any contracts, it is a good idea to photocopy them for your own reference and then return them safely to your legal company via registered post or by hand.

1 Conveyancer gains an instruction

- This normally happens when you agree a sale. The estate agent writes a letter to you and the buyer, giving details of both your legal representatives. No legal representative can work for the same buyer or seller.
- Once done, the full conveyancing process begins.
- If you have instructed your conveyancer before this time, steps 2–4 should be done. You can then move to draft contract stage (step 5) much quicker. The letter allows your conveyancer to know whose name to put on the contract and where to send it.

At this stage, some companies ask for part of the fee for any payments they need to make. Make sure this is deducted from the final bill.

2 Authorisation and application for the property deeds

- These are normally held by your mortgage lender or, if the property is owned outright, kept in a safe place (with the bank or a legal practice). This step can really eat up time – up to six weeks. It is dependent on the lender sending the deeds to your conveyancer.

3 Property information and fixtures and fittings forms

- Read carefully and complete accurately, even if the answer is 'don't know'. They help ensure the buyer is buying what you have said is for sale and that there are no outstanding issues that could affect the buyer.
- It's best to get the form filling over with as quickly as possible. Don't rush it, but don't put it off.
- **Property information form:** Asks questions about the property boundaries, which can be checked against information held at the Land Registry. It also asks about any disputes you may have received about your property and neighbours.
- **Fixtures and fittings form:** Forms the basis of what you are selling over and above the walls and other 'non moveables'. Fittings and fixtures include things like lights, door furniture, curtains, carpets and bathroom fittings, and outdoor things such as sheds or greenhouses.
- Think about what you are happy to leave behind. If you feel you should get money for something, such as a washing machine, cooker, fridge or freezer, say so.
- If you take something that you said you were leaving and the buyer wanted it (e.g. a dishwasher or wooden toilet seat), you may have to return or replace it.

- **Supplemental information and utilities questionnaire:** Some legal firms expect you to complete this form and if you are also buying a property, it's important for your vendor to do the same.

- It asks about things like your boiler, utilities, council tax, wiring, alarm system, and can save everyone a lot of time and trouble during the move by notifying the other party of who they need to contact when they move in.

4 Deeds received

- This is an important step in the process as nothing can happen until the deeds are received.

- After a few weeks of instructing your conveyancer, check they have received the deeds (unless, of course, they have informed you already).

- Some mortgage lenders send a letter to ensure you are aware the deeds have been requested and sent – this is done for security, so keep this letter on file.

5 Draft contract sent to buyer's solicitor

- To prepare the contract, the deeds and forms need to have been returned to your legal representative. Remember that the longer this takes, the longer you wait for the draft contract to be sent.

6 Buyer's enquiries

- Usually the buyer's solicitor will have questions or queries on the contract or forms received. Your legal representative may need to speak to you or someone else to get an answer. Delay holds up the process, so be speedy in your replies.

7 Final contract signed by the client

- Once the contract is signed, it is sent to the buyer's solicitors for final checking. You may be asked more questions at this stage.

- The dates for exchange and completion are now agreed. Anyone can set the dates and you can set the ideal exchange and completion dates from the start of the conveyancing process. Some sales are dependent on being able to complete by a certain day, as people have to get their children into school or start a new job, for example. So, suggest a date that's best for you and give approximately two weeks between the exchange and completion date. Once everyone is in agreement, give the final date for the move to your solicitor, although sometimes an agent manages this agreement process for everyone.

8 Contracts exchanged

- This happens over the phone. Your legal company rings the buyer's and confirms both parties have signed copies of a duplicate contract. The buyer's deposit monies are banked in the legal company's account and a date of completion is set. You now have a legally binding agreement and the respective contracts are posted to the other legal companies.

9 Deposit monies received

- When contracts are exchanged, the buyer has to pay a deposit to show commitment (unless you have 100% mortgage). The deposit goes to your solicitor and typically is 5% for properties under £99,999 and 10% for sales of £100,000+. However, the actual sum is negotiable. Your solicitor will advise you on the best amount as well as how to do this.

10 Contracts completed

- Each side confirms receipt of the other's contract and the money is transferred into your designated bank account. If you have a mortgage on the selling property, it will also be redeemed.

- The keys are handed to the estate agent or buyer only when this has happened. It is extremely important, no matter how much pressure you are under, that you do not give the keys to the new owner before your solicitor has confirmed the money is in the bank. A sale is not a sale until money has changed hands.

- It may be useful to let the estate agent have the keys so you are not put under emotional strain if the buyer is on your doorstep and the money's not.

HOW IT'S DIFFERENT IN
SCOTLAND

The buying and selling process in Scotland is different. Although there are fewer differences in selling than buying, it's worth mentioning where the two systems diverge. Here are some of the key points.

Be warned. Some properties are offered at a fixed price, so watch out for this. The reason for this appears to be to try and sell the property quickly without the fuss and bother of waiting for final bids.

ESTATE AGENTS VERSUS PROPERTY CENTRES

No matter where you live, you need to do your homework before you pick a good estate agent. The Scottish difference is that the companies that sell properties are not just estate agents but 'property centres'. These are typically a collective of solicitors who act as estate agents too. In theory they manage the whole process jointly, cutting out a lot of unnecessary and time-consuming communication. However, this does not always work as they often market their properties collectively with individual legal representatives managing the sale.

WHAT'S DIFFERENT?

Although the process of getting to the point of sale is more or less the same, the major differences are the valuation and the single blind bid auction system. On a property's initial valuation, the asking price in Scotland is called a guideline price and is often set low by agents so that as many buyers as possible are attracted. Typically the final price is higher (this can be above 10%). So to sell your property in Scotland:

- Do the same research as normal (see page 13), but remember your maximum and minimum price will be influenced by a guideline price, not an asking price.
- When you interview the property centre and selling agent, you need to ask two sets of questions: one for the estate agent (see page 23), the other for the conveyancer.
- Be prepared for a potential buyer to seek a survey ahead of making an

THE OFFER STAGE

This is where you see the most significant difference between Scotland and the England/Wales experience and is referred to as the single blind auction bid system. Rather than wait for viewers to make offers, there is a set time and date for people to make their bids. Usually it is set for a weekday at about 12 noon. It works like a sealed bid system, which sometimes operates in England and Wales (see page 52).

All of the bids are considered and passed to the seller by the property centre contact. It is then up to you – often with the centre's advice – to decide on which offer to accept. Who to accept is not just a money issue; it's also based on the completion date. If someone has not sold their property, then this is likely to be later than someone who has. In this case, a lower offer from an early completion date might prove the most attractive.

As the offers are made via a legal company and are binding if accepted, there is not so much of an issue as in England and Wales over whether a purchaser can afford to go ahead as they may be penalised if they pull out.

Everything else about selling a home remains the same until the offer stage (see page 50).

offer. This is because any offer (or bid) that somebody makes will be final and based on the true value of the property, taking into account any structural issues.

- Be warned: some properties are offered at a fixed price, so watch out for this as you may well be able to offer slightly less. The reason for the fixed price is either to try to sell the property quickly without the fuss of waiting for final bids or because the property has not attracted enough interest to generate a sale

LEGAL PROCESSES

For the legal process of selling, there are two main differences. First, the agent and solicitor is in one package. Second, but most importantly, when the potential buyers give the bids and one has been accepted, this effectively moves the process straight to the exchange stage. This is often why it is seen as a better system and for sellers it probably is. But if you're the buyer, it can be expensive since you may have to pay for more than one survey and make several attempts before your bid is finally accepted. Completion happens in the same way as in England and Wales.

RECEIVING **OFFERS**

Hopefully, if everything is going well and you have had regular viewings – and some second viewings – you should be soon receiving one or more offers. I am often asked how many people need to view a property before you get an offer. This is a difficult one to answer as the first person who walks through your door might be the one – or you could be waiting until person number fifty steps through. It just depends on who is looking to buy at the same time your property is for sale. People make offers on a property when they are keen to buy. Understandably, the strength of the offer will depend on:

- How much they really want your property
- Whether other properties exist that they would be equally happy to buy
- How much they can afford and can actually spend on the property.

WHEN THE OFFER COMES IN

There are three scenarios you may confront after you receive an offer:

- At the asking price. Normally people readily accept an offer at the asking price. However, there is often a niggle in the back of your mind: 'Could have I got more, especially if the property's only been on the market for a short time?' No matter, remember you do not have to accept the offer immediately.
- Just below. There may be room for manoeuvre nearer to the asking price. It just depends on how much the buyer can afford and whether there are any other properties they can offer on if you reject them.

QUICK TIP

At the beginning of this book I wrote about the need for emotional detachment. Applying this at the offer stage is extremely important. One way to help you do this is to agree both your ideal and bottom prices. Make sure these are the same as the maximum and minimum prices you discussed with the agent.

- Far below. It is easy to take offence at this stage, but try not to. Remember, the buyer might be offering low because they genuinely cannot afford to pay more but like your home and are hoping you can sell at a lower price. The potential buyer may also think your asking price is too high compared with other properties on the market. Also, the potential buyer may be in a strong position and hope to bag a bargain.

Once you have an offer, ask the estate agent:

- Is the buyer a cash buyer (does not have to sell a property to buy yours)? They could be renting, first-time buyers, buying a second home or buying to let.
- What does the agent think about the offer? If it were his/her property, would the offer be good enough to take?
- Will this offer help get other interested parties to make a bid? If yes, you can plan with the agent what to do next.
- Can the buyer afford your property? Was the offer above or below what the party originally said he/she was willing to pay? If it's above the original offer, the party may not be able to get the needed cash together to purchase.

In addition, what is happening in the market can also influence what you do next. If the market is moving fast, you may get more offers. If it is slow, offers can take longer and require careful consideration.

In the end, only you can decide to accept or reject an offer. For example, you may want to move quickly because you've already found a new property and need to sell quickly, or you would like the money in the bank so you will be in a better position to buy.

Whatever the offer, you have three options:

- Say, 'Yes' and agree how long you want before completion. Four weeks is fast, six to eight is good, but anything longer than that is beginning to be a drag.
- Say, 'Thanks, but ...' it is happening too quickly or the offer price is not what you want and you would like to wait a few weeks to see if you receive other offers.
- Say, 'Thanks, but I really want ...' the potential buyer to consider your minimum or ideal price.

WHAT IF THERE ARE SEVERAL OFFERS?

If you receive several offers, you're in a great position. First, you are likely to get your maximum price, as long as the buyer is able to proceed. But multiple offers are also a bit tricky as someone is going to get hurt and have their offer rejected. Your estate agent is also in a difficult position at this stage. They are legally not allowed to tell each buyer what the other has offered. This is to avoid pretend figures being given to potential buyers, which makes it difficult for buyers to know how much to offer.

If you are in this situation, take the offer from the buyer in the strongest position and if this is a lower offer, ask them to reconsider meeting your price. If everybody is in a strong position, take the offer from the people you would prefer to sell your property to. If you really can't decide, go for a sealed bid. This is similar to what happens in Scotland all the time (see page 49). Offers in a sealed envelope are given to the agent on a certain day at a certain time. The figures are revealed after the deadline and you choose which one you want – normally the highest one. This isn't my preferred way to buy or sell a property, but it does help you to make an impartial and unemotional decision.

THE FINAL **PRICE**

Remember, the buyer's mortgage lender may not agree to the purchase until a structural problem is fixed, particularly if they believe it impacts on the value of the property.

Once you and your agent have agreed an offer, you will be asked by the agent for details of your legal representative (assuming you haven't already given this). Then a letter is sent to you, your solicitor, your buyer and their solicitor notifying every one of each other's names and addresses and confirming the accepted price. At this stage, concurrent with the legal process, normally a survey is undertaken by your buyer on your property.

Many people think the offer is the final price, but the buyer often waits until after the survey and valuation is completed to make the final offer. This is because a survey (see page 119) can bring to light problems you were unaware of and consequently affect the price.

So if the survey is rather negative, your agent will be told the details. It is important you understand what exactly has been found wrong with the property and how much the surveyor expects it to cost to put right, as well as what impact this will have on the offer price (if any). Depending on the verdict, your options are to:

- Stick with your price
- Offer to reduce the price to reflect the work needed on the main problem area(s)
- Offer to fix the problem(s) – if you think this is cheaper than reducing the price and if you believe the buyer may pull out and do not want to have the same thing happen again with a new buyer.

Whatever you do, don't forget to check if the survey you commissioned when you bought the property identified the same problem(s) when you bought the property. If it didn't, you may want to talk to your surveyor about it and ask him/her to check if it's a new problem or something they missed. You may be able to claim against them, especially if it is a serious issue such as a major structural defect.

TROUBLE SHOOTING

	What's your problem?	Who can help you?
During the sale	No viewings in the first few weeks	Estate agent (see page 15)
	First viewing, but no second	Estate agent (see page 15)
	Second viewings, but no offers	Estate agent (see page 15)
	Offer is within the first few viewings	Estate agent (see page 15)

What can be done?

- Your estate agent should be able to tell you why no one is viewing. They should let you know how many people have seen your details and then provide you with a reason why they did not view.

- If the problem is something you can fix relatively easily – such as the front of the house or garden is not attractive – then fix it. Get a new photo of the house for the details.

- Check the details for your home, too. Are they describing your property accurately and showing it in the best light or is something putting people off?

- Check with your agent(s) that they have buyers in your price range on their books or are promoting the property to the right group of people.

- If you are not getting agent feedback, pop in and see them. Ask them who has visited and what the feedback was when they talked to the prospective buyer afterwards.

- If they are not following up, ask them to do so and agree a fixed day each week when they will give you feedback.

- If the feedback is that there is a problem that you could fix without too much trouble, then do so. If not, you may need to discuss reducing your price to help entice more second viewings. This could be tested on previous viewers as it might encourage them to come back.

- Once you have discovered why no one's biting, you may be able to fix it or you may just have to wait for a buyer looking for a certain type of property that just might be yours. Or you may need to adjust the price.

- If there is too much competition or it's a particularly slow time, take the house off the market if you are not desperate to move and put it back on when things have picked up or are less competitive.

- If the offer made means you can achieve your own objectives in moving, then consider it. But you may consider adding some conditions for accepting, like you want a quick sale.

What's your problem?	Who can help you?
Once the offer has been made and accepted		
You have not heard from your legal company after having instructed them on the sale	Estate agent (see page 15) Legal company (see page 40)
The buyer's solicitor is raising problems that may take a while to resolve	Legal company (see page 40)
All the paperwork is done but no date set for exchange/completion	Legal company (see page 40)
The buyer's mortgage offer falls through	Estate agent (see page 15)
During exchange and completion		
There are problems getting the contracts back from the buyer's solicitor	Legal company (see page 40) Estate agent (see page 15)
The forms or contracts are taking a long time to be sent between the buyer, their solicitor, your solicitor and you	You or your estate agent (see page 15) or legal company (see page 40)

What can be done?

- Call and ask what the problem or hold up is. Have some questions in mind like, 'Have you received the documents you need?', or if you need documents first, ask when they are to be sent.

- You could also ask what are the actual stages of the sale and what you (and the legal company) are expected to do at each stage (see page 44).

- Agree a method and timing for regular updates.

- Some issues raised during the legal process can be quickly resolved by taking out a specific type of insurance called Title Insurance. This protects the buyer from lack of planning permission information, papers not being signed, anything that a local search didn't show and so on. It can satisfy the buyer's legal company that it is safe to proceed. The legal company should advise you on what to do.

- You may have to help fund the insurance, but usually this is less than a few hundred pounds, so can be worth it if it means the sale can proceed swiftly and successfully.

- If you have a date you would like to exchange and complete by, then ask either the agent or your solicitor to see if it is possible to achieve these dates and gain everyone's agreement.

- There is little you can do, but find out and make sure you understand exactly why the mortgage fell through. Even when a company makes a provisional offer, there can be many reasons why they do not finalise the mortgage offer.

- Talk to your own financial advisor to gain verification of the reason(s) you are being given. As long as you are happy that the reason can be sorted out with another company, it should be relatively easy for your buyer to organise another mortgage within a couple of weeks.

- You could put a time limit on how long you are prepared to wait for the buyer to arrange an alternative or find another mortgage supplier.

- You need to find out what's the problem. Once you know why the contract has not been returned you can take specific action. Is it because the solicitor does not return calls, have documents been faxed and not received or lost in the system/post? You might even consider a personal visit to the buyer's solicitor by your agent or legal representative (as long as it's local).

- It may be that the buyer's solicitor has too much work to do and is not prioritising your buyer's work, so everyone – from the buyer to the agent and your legal company – needs to try to chase them. You could even threaten to pull out of the deal unless specified deadlines are agreed to.

- Paperwork has to pass from solicitor to vendor to your solicitor to buyer's solicitor and then the whole round begins again. At any stage in this passing around of documents, questions may arise and need answering. Remember these are draft contracts until approved, so things can be rewritten, added or deleted at any stage.

- Don't post things if it's critical to move quickly: either deliver in person (if local) or use a courier. Fax or electronic methods of transfer may or may not be appropriate. You may want to sort this out before you start. Remember, the quicker everyone, including the legal representatives, sees documents, the faster the process. So if everyone is relying on the post, it could take a few days for documents to be sent/arrive.

SECTION TWO

BUYING
A HOME

Buying a home seems in the beginning an exciting adventure, but it can soon become a time-consuming and seemingly endless task. Whatever type of property you are looking for, it is quite a lot to expect the exact home, in the perfect condition for your requirements and in the ideal location to be available at the price you are happy to pay – and all just at the time you are looking to buy. What makes this even less likely is that, on average, people move once every seven years, yet we only typically take three to five months to buy a property.

In this section we guide you through how to research the market and identify your wants and needs, while checking you can afford what you are looking for. There is also an explanation of the key stages of the buying process so that you can stay one step ahead of everyone and secure the home of your dreams.

WHY **BUY?**

Unlike many other European countries, UK residents prefer to buy their own home rather than to rent. This has not always been the case. In 1945, only 40% of the population owned their own home. But by 2003 – just over 50 years later – this had reached 68 per cent.

This culture of owning your own home coupled with the fact that more people live alone before they marry, an increased divorce rate and the rise of buying a second home means there simply are not enough houses being built to accommodate the growth in demand. This helped prices to soar in the late 1990s and into the beginning of 2000. Despite the increases, the vast majority of us are still keen to buy our own home. Many hope it will be able to replace any future pension deficits, too.

But buying a property can be a lengthy and expensive process, full of pitfalls and stress. One in three sales fall through after an offer has been made – after you've already spent money on legal preparation, mortgage help and a survey. This is a hard fact, but one that still does not deter us in our desire for ownership.

This chapter is designed to guide you through the many decisions you need to make when buying a property and to help you make them with as much assurance as possible. Don't forget that preparation can lessen the stress as well as help you to avoid problems. You can do a lot of research that will help you make better decisions and there are many sources of information that you can call on to ensure your move goes smoothly. So settle back. There are lots of hints and tips to help you, especially when things are not quite going according to plan.

BUYING VERSUS RENTING

To make an informed decision about buying or renting, you need to weigh up the pros and cons of both options. For some, renting can be a quick

QUICK TIP **If you have bought wisely and prices rise, you could earn yourself some tax-free cash when you sell. You can then use this money to buy something bigger, use the extra cash for something you've always wanted, or, later in life, use it to finance your retirement.**

and cheap option in the short term, but buying can be a good investment if house prices continue to increase.

OWNING YOUR OWN HOME

There can be many benefits of owning your own home. For one thing, ownership can give you freedom. You can come and go as you please. All the fixtures and fittings are yours, as well as the décor and any other changes you make. You are answerable only to yourself (and your neighbours).

However, buying a property will not always pay dividends. Like most investments, property prices can go down as well as up. In the early 1990s, some people who bought properties suffered from negative equity – when the home they bought turned out to be worth less than the mortgage they owed on the property. With the help of hindsight, many people may have preferred to rent instead of buying at the market peak.

Remember, too, that it can be hard work to find the right property at a price you can afford. Ownership ties you down to one place and makes it harder to move somewhere else if you have a new job, an addition to the family or decide to move in with a partner or get married.

Other possible negative consequences include:

- What if you don't really know the area where you are buying? In the longer term it may not deliver what you hoped for. New neighbours might move in, the road might get busier, new developments and other changes may take place that make you want to move.
- Personal reasons or simply changes in the area may mean that you decide soon after moving that you need (and want) to sell again. So back to square one. You now have to face the costs of selling and buying once again.

WHAT MAKES A GOOD OR BAD INVESTMENT?

If you want to buy a property with the idea of making money, not just to provide a roof over your head, you need to work even harder to ensure you buy the right place at the right price.

As with any investment, the first step is to decide the time frame. How long do you intend to stay in the property and how much do you want the property to increase in value over that time? Add in the cost of buying, selling and funding any mortgage, insurance and other costs. Now you need to become a property investment specialist and for your head, not your heart, to rule.

UNDER-PRICED AREAS

Whatever the area, road or property type, there is always a price limit that people will pay for an individual property. When choosing a property as an investment, you need to carefully research everything about the area, the road and the property you are looking to buy. If you intend to make money by refurbishing or extending a property, you must make sure that you know the most that you are willing to pay for the property, the costs for improvements and the final price you can sell it at. This way you know that you will make a profit. All of your decisions must be considered against what you do, how much you spend and the increased value that the changes make.

Areas where house prices are below true market value are often called property hot spots. These are hard to find unless you know an area well. Trying to identify them is down to a combination of research and luck. The key factor likely to create a property hot spot is new investment in the area that results in attracting more people and so pushes up property prices. For example, this might come from the government creating special incentives for companies to move to the area, therefore creating

QUICK TIP

Remember, if you purchase your property on the hope
that planning permission or changes are made, you run
the risk of it not happening. Wait until it's certain, if you can.

more employment; or from a large business relocating; or a new transport
link, such as a motorway, train station, tram or other route, as well as a
new upmarket housing development.

There are a variety of ways of finding out about these changes. You
could read commercial publications and spend time poring over the
planning applications at the local council or gaining information from
your local Regional Development Agency.

Typically, when property prices rise or fall in an area, however big or
small, these increases or decreases will ripple out to the surrounding
towns and villages as people seek to move further away from or closer to

MAKING A **WISH LIST**

When people first look to buy a property, they often start out with an assumption of how many bedrooms they want and then see what it might cost. To me this is jumping the gun a bit. Buying a house is probably one of the biggest purchases or investments you will make. So rather than look at how much properties cost, why not first think about the way you live your life in relation to your home?

For example, what is it you like about your current home? What is it you don't have now but want from a new home? This exercise is not just about what you want, but also about what you really need. So read through these questions, think about the answers and see if your needs and wish list are very different.

WHY CREATE A WISH LIST?

- **Everyone agrees on what is important** to everyone else involved in the move. Unless you have an unlimited budget, there may be compromises you need to make.

- **Knowing your 'must haves' is helpful.** You may need to prioritise features according to your budget. The clearer you are about what you must have compared with what would be nice, the easier it will be for any estate agents helping you find a property.

- **A detailed brief for your agent** makes it easier for them to send you to properties that you are likely to want to buy. They may also tell you that what you want is impossible in a particular neighbourhood or within the price range you've given, so you may need to go back to your lists and start making some hard choices.

- **You can take a 'reality check'** by putting some figures against the list and see exactly what you can financially afford. There are two types of finances to consider:
  - The cost of buying a home, which involves fees such as legals and surveys.
  - The running costs associated with moving to a new home. These may involve increased mortgage and utility payments.

Where do you want to live?

- What type of area do you want to live in?

- You might be sure of where you want to live, but what about the rest of the family?
  - Will moving to a different type of area affect your daily routine?
  - Out in the sticks: no neighbours, no local amenities.
  - In the city: lots of action, lots of noise.
  - Suburbs: good for schools, local amenities.

What type of property do you want to live in?

- Being sure on this can help narrow down where you look for properties.
  - Older property: lovely character but maybe hidden costs or restrictions.
  - New build: you're the first to live there, but when will it be finished?
  - Unusual: you may want to live on a houseboat, a folly, convert a barn, but what things do you need to consider that are different to a normal purchase?

What condition do you want the property to be in?

- You may initially like the idea of renovating a home, but are you happy to replace kitchens, bathrooms or floors?

- If you agree that you are happy to view properties in a poor condition, does that mean you will do structural work or just painting?

- Or are you prepared to pay a premium for somewhere in excellent condition but if it doesn't exist, are you prepared to pay less and then get someone in to do the work?

Travel times and destinations

- Living in the countryside might seem a good idea to begin with, but what if it means hours on public transport or stuck in the car? You need to identify your regular journeys

and what you consider a reasonable amount of time:
  - Work: half an hour each way or more; what's acceptable?
  - School: do you need the school run or can the children all walk or take public transport instead?
  - Amenities and leisure activities: how far to the nearest supermarket, hairdresser, doctor, golf club, video rental?
  - Public or private transport: congestion is increasing, but is public transport better?
  - Regular visits: are you prepared for longer journeys to see people or keep appointments?

What facilities do you need?

- If you have children you may want to get home at a reasonable time. Or if you go to work early and return late, having late opening local shops might be essential. If you enjoy a drink on a Friday and Saturday night, are you happy to get a taxi home or does the entertainment need to be on your doorstep?

- Clubs and associations: are your interests catered for in the new area; will they be better or worse than now?

- Health: is it important to be near a doctor and hospital or can you live with them further away?

- Outdoor facilities: do you use local parks or other facilities much and do you want more?

What accommodation do you want?

Having a clear idea of what you need and want helps you give a good brief. Make sure you know:

- How many reception rooms, bedrooms (double or single), bathrooms you need.

- Does any room need to be a certain size; does your favourite furniture fit?

- Do you need a garden big enough to play in or land to accommodate a horse or other pets?

- Garage or off-street parking: can you leave your car(s) on the street or does your insurance require them to be parked off-street?

CHECKLIST OF INCIDENTALS

✔ Decoration

✔ New furniture and/or soft furnishings

✔ New kitchen appliances

✔ Plumbing or electric work required (for example, refitting your satellite dish)

✔ Storage

✔ Postal redirection

✔ Overnight accommodation (your move may not happen in one day)

✔ Club or association fees

✔ School fees (if private)

✔ New (different) school uniforms

MAKE SURE YOU HAVE YOUR CASH READY

Don't forget that whether you are selling an existing property or not, you will have to have a certain sum of money put to one side to fund the purchase. You can't rely on receiving money from your mortgage lender or from a sale of property before you need to put money down on your new property.

The main up-front costs are legal and survey fees (see page 72) and the deposit at the exchange stage. If you are buying a new build property off-plan, you are usually required to make a deposit 28 days before completing the purchase. This amount varies, but can be as much as 10% of the purchase price (see page 111).

Believe it or not, some sales have fallen through because the buyer did not realise cash up front was required at the time of exchange (see page 45). The amount of the deposit is agreed between you and your buyer through your legal representatives.

ON-GOING COSTS OF
FINANCING A HOME

Once you have a list and a budget for the physical costs of moving into a property, you then need to work out if your on-going costs are going to increase. When you want to buy a bigger flat or house, you need to make sure you can cover any likely increased costs. However, a bigger house doesn't always equate to more costs. You may be moving to a larger property in a cheaper area, so you might save instead.

Either way it is essential to have an idea of how much your monthly and annual costs will increase to make sure you can afford the new commitment. Most people just think of the monthly mortgage increasing. But that's only one part of financing a home. You don't need to have a property in mind to start the calculations, just use your current bills and overall financial situation to model the expected increase. Without this reality check, you may commit to a property which you later struggle to fund. To work out your on-going costs, see the chart overleaf.

DOES IT ALL ADD UP?

Now you should have a list of all the costs involved in buying (and selling) a property. You also know what money you have available compared with what you need to pay. Finally, if you have a property to sell you will know if any money will be left over. Next you need to investigate what mortgage you can afford and will be best for you. Over recent years the way this is calculated has changed in two ways.

It used to be relatively easy to work out how big a mortgage you could be given. It used to be two-and-a-half times joint salaries or three times one salary – whichever was the larger figure. But with the different types of mortgage that are now available (see page 100) this has changed. Mortgages are based on affordability. In many cases this makes sense as a couple who earns £20,000 each but have no children or no cars could

FINDING A **HOME**

If you are moving to a new area, the more research you do the better. Even somewhere a few miles down the road might throw up lots of issues you need to be aware of and have a chance to think through.

LOCAL PAPERS

The best starting point for information is from local newspapers or magazines. Many of these may also have Internet sites available. The press will let you know what's going on that's good, bad and ugly. But remember, even the local free publications may dwell on the unsavoury and forget to mention the really good things.

The worst thing that can affect property prices, sometimes reducing them by up to 18%, is often found to be next door (i.e. a bad or troublesome neighbour) or the fact that the property backs onto a rundown or derelict property. Either avoid these situations or make sure you gain a good reduction in the price.

Usually there are two levels of newspaper – a main one sold across the area/county such as the *Evening Standard* in London or the *Evening Post* in Nottingham and purely local papers such as the *Surrey Comet* or *Newark Advertiser*. If you are moving a long way and don't know anyone who can send copies of the local papers to you and you can't use the Internet, you could ask a local newsagent to send papers (obviously paying them for this service). This gives you access to the weekly property listings as well as the main headlines and other local news. Pay particular attention to the letters page. You'll often find out about the main local issues and even planned major projects (including possible hospital or school closures) that could affect your decision to live in the area.

LOCAL COUNCIL

There is a wealth of information held by the local and district councils. Fortunately, most of this is available via the web. The things to look out for are strategic plans on, for example, transport, communication, environmental issues and schooling. If you have a child who has special needs, or one of the family needs constant medical attention, then check

MAKING CONTACT

Local government and council information:
www.upmystreet.co.uk

Useful cost of living calculator:
www.npower.co.uk

Information and links to village locations across the UK:
www.ukvillages.co.uk

Site for checking flooding, radon and other nasties:
www.homecheck.co.uk

A government site similar to Homecheck:
www.environment-agency.gov.uk

out the types of schools and hospitals in the area. You can also go to the local council offices and ask to speak to someone about your concerns and get answers for the questions that are important to you. Ask for recent planning applications, too, so you know if any new developments – good or bad – may be coming into the area.

Don't forget to check other information such as crime statistics and council taxes. If you can, pick up a local copy of the telephone book, which will give you a good idea of what's available in almost every area.

TOURIST BOARD

Most areas have a nearby tourist board that can give you a good insight into what there is to do at weekends or during school holidays. They can also highlight areas that might seem idyllic outside of the tourist season, but can be swamped in the summer. If the tourist information staff have worked in the area for a while, they may be able to answer more questions you have as well as point you to other organisations that might be useful.

INTERNET

There are some national websites that can help you find more information about places (see Making contact, above). But there may be some good local websites that are even better suited to your requirements. Some of these will be linked to local newspapers and government, others may be advertised in the local paper (like the local chamber of commerce or entertainment and other interest groups). Alternatively, do a general search to find more information via the web.

QUICK TIP When searching for properties on the Internet only put in your must haves, not your wish list, as you will get a better range of properties returned.

ESTATE AGENTS

In most areas there will be at least one independent agent that will have been around for the last 10 to 20 years. If they have a surveying practice or commercial division and have up to five offices in the local area they can be incredibly informative. The staff in these offices typically live around the area and know it well. As long as you pick your time correctly, agents are usually happy to sit down with a map, go through your likes and dislikes and suggest areas to start looking – and just as importantly ones to avoid. Some will even drive you around – especially if you show you are a serious buyer and can view properties immediately. In this way, you can sit back and take everything in rather than worry about where on earth you are and argue over who's better at map reading!

FRIENDS AND FAMILY

Don't forget them; they are a great resource. Contact as many people as possible to help you find the local newspapers, council and Internet sites. If someone you know has lived in the area, they may be very useful to you. They will know the inside story, have an idea of good and bad areas and hopefully of the better schools and amenities. Remember that everyone's taste is different. So always check things against your list of likes and dislikes and don't rely entirely on someone else's view.

COMPARING AREAS

Once you have a list of areas that you like the sound of, you can start prioritising them against your must have/wish list. Whatever your priority, be it distance to work, schools or low crime rates, you can use the research sources highlighted in this section to help you. Once you have identified which areas suit your needs, you will need to find out if the

Even if you are head over heels about a property, check what the insurance premiums are likely to be on your property, possessions and car.

Beware of idyllic situations such as properties backing onto rivers. Remember the nightmare scenario that may accompany such a position – floods, for example. Think about how devastating a flood can be and that it takes months to get rid of the effects – and you may have to go through the same thing the next year. Check with the locals. Sometimes flood information is available by postcodes. You can then see if your house and road is affected or not.

type of property you want exists. For example, trying to find an old property in a new town such as Telford would be quite hard. But the surrounding villages or an older nearby town might have the type of property you want. The downside may be a longer journey to work. You'll need to balance the pros and cons.

If you find a town that you love, it is always heartbreaking then to discover you can't afford to live there. But think through why you want to live there. Is it a really brilliant shopping centre, or does it have great pubs or schools? Now look how far out you would have to live to find somewhere cheaper and still make the town you love an acceptable distance away. For example, you may find that by living on the edge of the town, prices are lower. In London, living in one postcode rather than another can substantially reduce the price of property. But if you can still use the amenities of the more expensive areas on a daily or weekly basis, you've achieved your dream home and lifestyle.

Sometimes, by visiting areas regularly, you find that although you love it, so do many other people. In fact, it may get very congested, so it is better to be able to get there by park-and-ride schemes, train, tram or priority bus routes. The school catchment area may include places outside the immediate one you are looking at. By talking to and visiting the school you may discover there are other areas you could look at or ways that you may be able to have your children attend the school you want while still living in a less expensive neighbourhood. By delving into an area at this level, you may completely change your perspective and find that with some compromising, you can have it all.

LOCATING YOUR
PROPERTY

All of the research, lists and tables I have described should now start to pay off as you search for properties. If you know the area, or even specific roads you want to move to, the process is much simpler. There are a variety of ways you can start narrowing down your search.

PROPERTY INTERNET SITES

One way to narrow the search may be judicious use of the Internet. With the added advantage of being able to search when you want to, initially you may find this option is the best. However, websites can be good or bad. Check to see how often a site is updated and how many different agents advertise properties on each site. When it comes to your personal search, they are only as good as the number of properties they have for sale in the area you are looking at, the type of property you want, and at the price at which you want to purchase.

It is really important not to stick to one portal, but to use several. Some agents own different portals and exclusively advertise on one site only. Others are owned privately or by newspaper companies that sell advertising space to estate agents. The best use of property portals is to narrow down the estate agents that sell the type of property you are looking for, in your price range and in the area you want to live. A list of key property portals is given opposite.

ESTATE AGENT DIRECTORIES

Estate agent directories is another way of searching. These will give you information based on the area (or postcode) you want to research as well as the agent's contact details and a map to find them. As estate agents come and go on a yearly basis and as they cover different postcodes around their area, it is hard to keep an up-to-date list of which agents cover the exact locations you are looking for. Estate agent directories are getting better at this. Some of the better ones are:

- www.email4property.co.uk
- www.estateangels.co.uk
- www.yell.co.uk
- www.thomweb.co.uk

Many of the property portals now allow you to search their database of estate agents as well as properties.

Many estate agents had hoped that advertising on the Internet would replace newspaper adverts. Not so. Many find they need to be seen in both places. Because the Internet sites do not always update regularly, the local weekly property newspapers are still one of the best ways to find properties and estate agents. They need to be a major part of a buyer's research. Many of these newspapers – even the free ones – also have Internet sites, so you need to check which ones do and look to see if they update their website as often as they do their paper – or indeed more often.

MAKING CONTACT: KEY PROPERTY PORTALS

Site	Controller	Other
www.assertahome.co.uk	Asserta Holdings Ltd	Other agents pay to advertise their properties
www.rightmove.co.uk	Countrywide (various estate agencies) Connells Bradford & Bingley Halifax	Other agents pay to advertise their properties
www.naea.co.uk	National Association of Estate Agents (NAEA) for their members	Only NAEA offices can advertise
www.primelocation.co.uk	The 'top' market agents such as Hamptons, Lane Fox, Humberts	Other agents pay to advertise their properties
www.fish4homes.co.uk	A local and national newspaper	Companies that advertise their properties in their papers can advertise here

The best use of the papers to a buyer is that they help you research how many properties of your type, favoured location and price are on the market. Most people search for properties that are up to 10% above the highest amount they could offer, mainly in the hope that if they make an offer, the seller will accept less.

Newspapers also help you to narrow down the agents that are most likely to gain instructions for your 'must have and wish list' home. You can then register with each one.

To save time, many of the Internet sites allow you to contact agents via email and register your requirements at the same time. This is a good service but not all estate agents respond, so you may still have to call to be registered.

UPS AND DOWNS OF
PROPERTY PRICES

When buying or selling a property, you need to gain an understanding of what drives prices up or down. The main factor is how many buyers are chasing the properties that are for sale. If there are more buyers than sellers, so the prices tend to rise. If there are more sellers than buyers, prices tend to fall. However, it is not just that simple as people buy and sell completely different property types: new and old, studio flat or 20-bedroom mansion, those in good condition and ones that need lots of investment, to name but a few! If buyers all want houses and only flats are up for sale, then the price of the flats may go down and the price of houses that come onto the market may increase. Or if you want to live on a certain road and many others do too, you may have to compete on price to secure the property.

The best effect on price is to be near a main line railway station – but not too near to hear the noise.

To get the property you want and achieve your must haves you may need to compromise on price and area or accept having to live near a main road or railway line.

A company called Hometrack, part of a group of companies that operate in the property market and issue monthly housing market surveys, polled their estate agents to identify local conditions that increase or decrease the price of properties. Although not a definitive piece of research, it does give you an idea of what to look out for and can help you compare properties you are interested in (see left).

PROPERTY UPS AND DOWNS

Upside (within 3 miles)

Up to 5%	Good amenities such as cinema/entertainment facilities, post offices and banks, sports and social clubs, restaurants and quality food stores
Up to 10%	Countryside and parks, top state schools and good transport links

Downside

Up to 5%	Mobile phone/telecom masts
Up to 10%	Local authority housing, railway line, prison, electricity pylons, poorly-rated comprehensive schools
More than 10%	Busy road, amenity and other waste dumps, flight paths, derelict land, smelly takeaways and late night establishments for drinking and music

BUYING A PROPERTY THROUGH
ESTATE AGENTS

However you find a property to buy, the vast majority (over 80%) of properties are sold via estate agents. So the better you know and work with them, the more likely you are to get the property you want.

Even though estate agents act on behalf of the vendor, those that sign up to a code of practice will look after anyone who registers and buys through them. Good agents recognise that treating buyers well is essential if they are to gain a sale. The really good ones also recognise a longer-term advantage if they treat you well – you may call and instruct them to sell your property later.

Put yourself in the estate agent's shoes for a moment. Something like half the people that register with them to buy never go through with it. Nevertheless, they still have to do all the work: get details prepared and sent out, follow up to see if they want to view a property, take them to viewings and continue to follow up on the vendor's behalf. Imagine if half of your work were a wasted effort. How would you feel? So, don't be too hard on estate agents. If you can show you are a serious buyer, you are much more likely to receive a good service and quality attention.

And don't be too hasty to reject all estate agents. Unlike in the States, there appears to be a real lack of trust between agents, buyers and even the sellers. Hopefully, having read these pages, you will better understand why agents ask the questions they do and do some of the things they do – even the things that irritate you.

BE SPECIFIC ON YOUR BRIEF

One of the most common 'dinner party' complaints by buyers is that agents send property details outside their brief: too expensive, too cheap, too few bedrooms, too many, no garden or one you don't want.

WHAT QUESTIONS AGENTS ASK AND WHY

When you register as a buyer, the first job for the estate agent is to validate you as a real buyer for themselves and for vendors. They do this by asking standard, key questions. Here are some of them. I can't stress enough the importance of being honest when answering any questions an estate agent may ask. If you are not honest it is likely that you will be found out at some stage and your offer may fall through, losing you the property you wanted.

- **Have you a property to sell?**
  The agent needs to work out if you are a potential future instruction (you might sell your house through them). Furthermore, the agent wants to find out if you are in a strong position to buy.

- **Are you a cash buyer?**
  The vendor will want to know this. If you are not a cash buyer and there are properties that need to be sold quickly, there is little point introducing you to those. If you are not in this position and went to view such a property, you would no doubt chastise the agent for wasting your time. Many people don't really know what cash buyer means. There are two types. A real cash buyer has an amount of money that is immediately accessible and equals the price of the property to be purchased. The second type of cash buyer has nothing to sell, but needs a mortgage to fund the purchase.

- **What stage is your sale at?**
  If you are selling a property, the agent will ask whether you have received an offer (in writing), if a survey has been done on your property, when you are expecting to exchange and complete contracts and how long your property has been on the market. This helps the agent assess if you really are intending to purchase and are not just having a look. It also helps them to judge how quickly you could make an offer and in what time frame you are likely to be able to sell your property. If you haven't had a viewing and the property is in their catchment area, they may try to gain your business from your agent.

- **Have you agreed or looked at obtaining a mortgage?**
  Most people assume agents ask this because they want to sell you a mortgage. Some do and may be targeted to do so, especially agents that are owned and have affiliation deals with finance companies.

The myth that estate agents hold properties back from buyers who don't look into getting their mortgage sometimes happens, but it is rare and if found out, the agent could be fined. The main reason agents ask this question is that if the buyer's finances are not checked, then how can the agent and vendor validate the ability of the buyer to purchase a property?

QUICK TIP **As you get more details and view more properties, work with the agent to help them understand what you like and dislike. Ring or email the agent with the pros and cons of the property and whether you would short list and view again.**

I have tried to get statistics from agents to find out how many people end up buying the same property they originally briefed the agent for. So far research from Townends Estate Agency, who have over 30 offices in Surrey, suggests that on average one in four buyers purchase something different from the brief they gave. Therefore, if they stuck rigidly to every buyer's brief they would not be giving every vendor the best opportunity to sell their property.

Thanks (or not) to technology, many agents have software that automatically matches potential buyers with new instructions. How good a match is down to the way in which they capture your wish list and must haves. Most seem to be able to define particulars such as number of bedrooms, other rooms, garden and other standard features as well as maximum and minimum price. But few are able to distinguish between old and new properties for example.

All you can do is try to be as specific as you can about what you want, what you don't want and what you would rather not have. Make this as clear as possible. Brief them on your must haves only and talk to them as you get details and go to viewings about what you liked and didn't like. Two key things to be careful about when briefing an agent are:

● What exactly are your must haves. For example, do your need a garage and, if so, why? If you have a dog, will you need a garden or to be close to a park?
● When you talk about rooms, be specific. For example, for bedrooms do you mean double or single? Is a bathroom upstairs essential, or if there were an en suite upstairs and a bathroom downstairs, would that be acceptable? Do any of the rooms need to be a certain size for furniture or other items you may have? If you specify the need for a garage does it have to be secure or would you consider a car-port or standing?

GETTING THE BEST OUT OF ESTATE AGENTS

Agents get paid and make their money by selling properties. In other countries – the US for example – agents are paid for both the sale and the purchase, on average 3% of both. This means that they earn nearly three times the commission for property purchase and sale that agents in the UK do. Anything you can do to help make their lives easier will make it more likely that you will get the best out of your agent:

● **Answer the agent's questions truthfully** and without restraint when you register with them.

● **Show you are a serious buyer.** Remember that the agent has to verify your financial status so hand over a copy of your MAP and offer to get your bank to confirm in writing that you have the funds to purchase a property.

● **Give a specific brief to the agent.** Unless the agent is sending you rubbish, look at the details you want and throw the rest away. Usually agents send property details out that are plus or minus 10% of the price range you give. They are normally quite good at sticking to the number of bedrooms, but will find wish lists and unusual requirements harder to manage.

You can go one step further **to ensure you only have the details you want** by requesting them from the Internet, or printing them off for yourself if they load the full sales particulars onto their Internet site. You can then call the agent weekly and ask them to **send you details of properties** that have just come onto the market and have not yet been loaded onto the net.

VIEWING PROPERTIES

It's a good idea to save yourself and everyone else's time by driving by properties you are interested in, just to confirm, if nothing else, that this is a place in which you would be happy to live. Obviously, if you do not live near the properties you want to view, this will be difficult if not impossible to do. Agents can, however, organise a selection of property viewings for you on one day if they are given a week-to-ten-days notice.

Unless there are unavoidable circumstances, do not cancel a viewing on the day as people are likely to have gone to a lot of effort to make sure they are available as well as to ensure the place is tidy. It also makes the agent look bad in the vendor's eyes if you cancel, so the agent won't be particularly happy with you either.

As in any working environment, agents have slow and nightmare days. Most completions happen on a Friday at the end of the month, so this is definitely a day to avoid contacting estate agents. A well-run office should be able to use the quieter days to get feedback to vendors and buyers. Talk to the agent about when new instructions are most likely to come in during the week and month and ask when it's best to contact them to discuss particular properties.

Ask if they have text or email alerts or other systems you can sign up to that allow you to know about new properties coming onto the market as soon as possible. Make sure the agent is aware that you can go to look at new properties speedily. Remember, early viewings when a property has just been put on the market make the agent look good. It also means you get the chance to see properties as soon as possible.

Finally, it is worth popping into the agents every couple of weeks and asking if anything else has come on the market, if instructions are increasing or decreasing, and if they are registering more buyers. This helps keep you in their mind as well as up to date on what is happening in the market that might affect your purchase.

REVIEW YOUR DECISION

Once you have decided that there are one or two properties that meet your needs, try to view the property you are most interested in at three different times during the day as well as at weekends or during the week. You don't need to go in every time; you may be able to get an idea of what you want to know simply by driving by. Doing this can alert you to potential unpleasant surprises you may only otherwise find out about after you move in.

You may want to add to this list, but some of the key things to do are:

The Royal Institute of Chartered Surveyors recommends you do not make an offer on property at auction unless you have already sold your own property. If you are successful in a bid, you effectively exchange contracts on the auction day and are committed to the sale.

- Check times for journeys that you regularly make. Just one additional busy junction or one less train may adversely effect your journey.
- If you are living near a school, check out how difficult parking and noise is around arrival and departure times.
- If there is a train line nearby, sit outside the house and work out what the level of noise is and find out the timetable. It might be an acceptable noise level during the day, but at night it may feel a lot louder. The same goes for any pubs, shops, petrol stations or other amenities that might affect noise levels. And don't forget to ask about flight paths for nearby airports.
- If you don't have on-street parking, visiting at different times of the day (early morning, late afternoon and night) will help you assess if you'll have parking problems. Having to park around the corner regularly may become irritating after a while.

BUYING AT AUCTION

Over 30,000 properties in the UK are sold at auction every year. To find out about auctions, look in phone directories, local newspapers, search on the Internet (see box, opposite) and contact local auction houses.

MAKING CONTACT

Through these websites you can locate auctions in your area:

www.propertyauction.com
www.eigroup.co.uk
www.rics.org/property_auctions

One of the advantages of buying at auction is that subject to contracts being completed, the property becomes yours within days or at the most a few weeks. You get access to some cheaper properties, which might have been repossessed or need work on them. The downside is you have to spend money on surveys, legal bits and pieces and other searches prior to the auction – and you may not end up owning the property.

TOP STEPS TO BUYING AT AUCTION

1 **Find out where and when** your next local property auction is.

2 **Go to two or three auctions** first to get used to them and see who else buys.

3 **Secure a catalogue** for the next auction.

4 **Identify properties** that meet your requirements.

5 **Visit each of the properties,** taking notes of the pros and cons.

6 **Ask the auctioneer** what information and details are available about the property you are interested in.

7 **Instruct a surveyor and a legal representative** to find out if there are any problems that you should know about or if there are any outstanding legal issues concerning the property.

8 **Ring the auction house** and register your interest. They can advise you of any updates or if the vendor is willing to consider an offer prior to auction.

9 **Prepare your deposit money and total financing** for the property well in advance. You will have to pay an average deposit of 10% by cheque on the auction day if your bid is successful.

10 **If your bid is accepted, organise building insurance** immediately as you are now liable if anything happens to the property.

FREEHOLD AND LEASEHOLD
EXPLAINED

You are likely to come across both freehold and leasehold properties when buying or selling a property. These terms describe the nature of the ownership of the property or home that is for sale. **Freehold** is associated mostly with houses and commercial buildings. It means you are buying both the property and the land as defined in the legal documents from the Land Registry.

Leasehold usually comes into play when purchasing commercial and retail premises and flats or houses that have been converted into separate units. It means you are buying the right to live in that property for a specified period of time but not the land on which the property is built.

THE ORIGINS OF FREEHOLD AND LEASEHOLD

- These terms have their origin in 1066 when William the Conqueror decided to take ownership of everything in sight. Once he owned all of the land, he was then in a position to give some of it away – either to a person or family forever or for a person's lifetime. This formed the basis for the two ways in which land and property is now owned: freehold and leasehold.

- The terms were formally defined and introduced in 1925 with the Law of Property Act.

- At the same time, the Land Registry Act was introduced, which required that all future sales and purchases to be registered, and ownership was then legally defined as leasehold or freehold.

FREEHOLD

- Freehold ownership is the stronger option and typically gives you more rights to do what you want to the property (subject to planning).

- With freehold, you have the right to occupation of the land for as long as you want.

LEASEHOLD

- With leasehold, you buy a property that is typically part of a building such as a flat or a semi-detached property, which is part of a larger building. The property is sold on a 'leasehold' basis and a length of time for the ownership is given, such as 99 years or 999 years. From the day you buy the property, this right of ownership decreases every year. If a lease has less than 85 years remaining then a mortgagee may require an extension to the lease.

- The key element of a leasehold is that you buy an agreed part of a freehold property to live in, such as a flat in a house or block of flats.

MAKING CONTACT

Lease Advice
Tel: **0845 345 1993**
Website: **www.lease-advice.org**
Email: **info@lease-advice.org**

Association of Residential Managing Agents
Tel: **020 7978 2607**
Website: **www.arma.org.uk**
Email: **info@arma.org.uk**

Both of these are independent organisations (Lease Advice is a government funded organisation) and can therefore help give impartial advice.

- Typically, the costs of upkeep are shared among the leaseholders and so leasehold properties usually come with more costs than freehold ones. These costs can include such things as:
  - Ground rent paid to the freeholder.
  - Service charges that vary.
  - Buildings insurance that is generally split between leaseholders within the property covered by the policy.
  - One-off investment costs such as a new roof.

- This is the main reason conveyancing for a leasehold property usually costs more. There are more things that need to be checked such as:
  - Who owns the freehold.
  - What rights has the owner to increase ground and service rent.
  - The necessity to obtain copies of the building insurance from the freeholder.
  - Finding out who is liable for alterations and other upkeep.
  - What rights and restrictions are placed on the leaseholder (for example, no pets, no sub-letting of rooms).

THE FUTURE OF LEASHOLD

- Many leasehold properties ran for 99 years, or could go for 999 years.

- However, as we are not far from being 100 years from the 1925 Act, which last modified leasehold regulation, the government is looking at introducing a new term, 'commonhold', to solve the issues being raised by current 'short lease terms' of say 30 years.

- This new classification would give leaseholders the right collectively to purchase the freehold and take over managing the building themselves.

- A collective purchase will hopefully help eliminate the issue of short leasehold contracts.

- It also has an additional benefit of giving the property upkeep control to the residents.

- This should prevent some of the horror stories we have all heard of such as sudden massive increases in rents and service charges or large sums of money being required to pay for building work.

NEW HOMES **DEVELOPMENTS**

There are many reasons why buying a new home can make purchasing a property straightforward and cost effective. First there is no emotion involved from the seller's perspective. All the developer wants to do is build and sell the properties at a profit. Unlike an independent seller, they have lots of properties to sell and are not in the process of buying another one. They also heavily compete with other local developments, so are more able to offer a competitive price.

If you have a small amount available for deposit, but enough to pay the on-going costs, some builders will help you with the deposit and the associated fees that go with it. They can afford to do this, as it is in their interest to promote a sale. If it is coming up to the end of a financial year, they may drop prices and do anything they can to close a few extra deals.

Second, by putting an offer in early during the building of the new homes, you may be able to influence the design and build of your property. Having this from the start can be far more cost effective than making changes once you are already in the property and is certainly less disruptive.

How nice too for a buyer to have a blank canvas on which to work, straight walls to hang pictures or tiles on. A new home also offers state of the art technology and is often highly energy efficient, therefore cutting down on utility bills.

Another reason to buy a newly built property is if you are struggling to sell your own home, they may be able to step in with a 'part-exchange scheme' and make you an offer on the property you are selling as well as assist you in buying their home.

PROS AND CONS OF BUYING OFF-PLAN

Pros

- Can be built to your specification and design
- May get a better deal
- Can be beneficial in a market where prices are increasing
- You have your pick of the plot
- There is no upward chain

Cons

- You won't see it until it's finished, so it may not live up to your expectations or be quite like the brochures
- Don't know who is going to live next door
- Problems caused if the builder runs out of money and cannot complete the development
- You need to produce a 10% deposit within days of signing, yet it could be months before you take possession of the property

DIFFERENCES WHEN BUYING A NEW HOME

When you agree to buy a new home, you typically have to pay the deposit within 28 days of signing the contract. Compared to a normal property sale, you are effectively moving to the exchange stage immediately and complete the purchase when the property is built and ready for you to move in.

Many builders now encourage people to buy off-plan – commit to the purchase prior to the property being built. In a rising market, this can save you money as opposed to buying when the development is ready to move into some months or even a year later. You may also gain a better price as your money helps recoup some of the money spent on building earlier. However, the downside for you is that you have to hand over your money early and the developer may not complete on the property when originally agreed.

Another perceived difference is that you don't need a survey (see page 119). But just because the home is new, it doesn't mean it is perfect. New homes should always be built to the latest building regulation standards. For example, new regulations over the years have meant that new build properties have been built in an energy efficient way. There should be guarantees for the windows, timber and damp proofing. The National Home-Building Council (NHBC) (see page 98) set up a 'warranty' that is issued to 85% of new build properties and is given following spot checks on the property, in theory, when it is finished.

However, an independent surveyor should always check the work of the builder. A completion agreement should be subject to the surveyor's report.

If you are expecting to purchase a new home, make sure you instruct a legal company who has a specialist knowledge of new home legals. They will be able to advise you better on contracts and issues raised from buying 'off-plan'.

QUICK TIP If buying off-plan, visit another site with similar properties on it and if you can talk to someone who lives there, you can find out what they think of the development and be able to flag up problems or issues they've encountered.

There are many horror stories of people who have had problems with newly built properties, such as flooding from dodgy plumbing and cracks appearing. Although the guarantees supply you with some reassurance that checks have been made, they do not cover everything. The NHBC can only act as a mediator if you have problems with builders. It cannot force them to rectify problems. The worst that can happen is that the builder is ejected from the NHBC scheme, which will not help to solve your problems.

Finally, there is that lovely show house. Don't be fooled; it is bound to look airy and spacious. The house you look at might be the best you can buy, not the minimum. You might find that what you are actually buying is the basic model, so check what is included in the purchase price and compare the difference between that and the show house specifications. Check if there are built-in cupboards or how much space you would need for them if they are not included. Rooms can look bigger without them.

NHBC SCHEME

The National Home-Building Council (NHBC) scheme is a **warranty, typically given for ten years.** The NHBC is a non-profit distributing company and is funded by the member developers. The council has developed a warranty for builders that is given to a property **following an NHBC employee inspection.** The NHBC estimates that 85% of new homes built in Britain are covered by this warranty.

In theory, the warranty is good news for buyers of new build properties as it checks the property for any defects before you move in. However, in practice, the checks are sometimes carried out too early in the build or are not thorough enough. If a problem does occur after you move in and is not rectified by the developer, the NHBC **can only mediate on your behalf**, they cannot force the developer to do anything and the worst 'penalty' they can impose is taking away their membership.

This is why you must **always have an independent surveyor** check a new build property before you complete on the contracts.

FINANCING **YOUR HOME**

Once you have found a house you want to buy, it is imperative that you double-check if you can afford it before you make an offer. There are five key elements to financing a home:

- Mortgage
- Buildings and contents insurance
- The deposit
- Life assurance
- Personal insurance plans

Many years ago, organising financing a home was simple. Mortgage applications were reviewed monthly and you had a choice between an 'interest only' or a 'repayment' mortgage. Rarely did you change your mortgage lender and any insurance associated with buying a property was then organised with the same company. Your mortgage was relatively simple to work out. It was three times the first salary plus one times the second, or two-and-a-half times the joint salary.

Over the last ten years, however, the mortgage market has changed beyond recognition. Choice, flexibility and variety have been added. Mortgages can be discounted, fixed or tracked. Interest can be calculated daily. Redemption penalties are disappearing, so you can pay off mortgages when you want, rather than waiting and paying more interest. Some flexible mortgages allow you to put all your money in one account.

Mortgages are now based on affordability. For example, if you earn £20,000 and have two children and two cars, you will be able to afford a smaller mortgage than a single person on the same salary. Insurance can be organised through separate companies, and you can choose whether to protect your mortgage payments from sickness or redundancy. You can even change your insurance every year to get the 'best deal'.

YOUR MORTGAGE

Hopefully you will already have a mortgage agreement in principle (MAP), in which case now is the time to finalise your finances with the property that you want to make an offer on. If you haven't got your MAP, sort it out as soon as possible (see page 77). There are two types of mortgage, which are repaid either on a repayment or an interest only basis.

REPAYMENT MORTGAGE

With a repayment mortgage, monthly payments to the lender consist of **interest and a part repayment** of the mortgage. For example, if you have a £100,000 mortgage, your monthly payments include a sum that covers the interest on the loan, plus a sum that goes towards paying the capital sum (the amount you borrowed). In the early years of a repayment mortgage, your monthly payments will mainly be paying off the interest of the loan with a small element going towards repaying the loan itself. In the later years, the reverse is true and the **majority of your monthly payments** will go towards repaying the loan. Repayments to the lender are higher than interest only loans and, at the end of the term, there will also be no other money left over.

INTEREST ONLY MORTGAGE

Under an interest only mortgage, monthly payments to the lender pay **only the interest owed on the loan**, not the loan capital itself. So on a £100,000 mortgage your monthly payment will not pay off the mortgage itself. With this type of mortgage, you have to make your own arrangements to ensure there are sufficient funds available to repay the mortgage at the end of the term. To do this you could sell your house and use the money from the sale to repay the loan. Anything left over would be yours to keep. However, it is more common to arrange a **separate savings scheme** such as an individual savings account (ISA) or an endowment plan. These are designed to provide the amount of money you need to purchase the property outright or to sell it, keeping any proceeds.

One of the main disadvantages of this type of arrangement is that your savings scheme may not provide the return needed to repay the mortgage. It would then be your responsibility to make good any shortfall. As this type of mortgage requires a **savings plan** to sit alongside the loan, it's important to discuss your attitude towards risk with an independent financial adviser.

SAVINGS PLANS FOR INTEREST ONLY MORTGAGES

A wide variety of saving schemes are available. Financial advisers (independent – those not tied to a particular bank, building society or product range – or others) may be able to advise you as to what would be the best mix for you. Some of the more popular options are explained in the following pages and should give you initial information of the pros and cons of each. You may already have invested in some of these saving

With the onset of the Internet, we can now choose from hundreds of sites – each of which have hundreds of finance deals to choose from to help us get the cheapest financing 'at the touch of a button'. Well, almost!

plans independently of your mortgage. It is therefore important that you work through your financial options and estimate future cash flows (money going out as well as coming in) before deciding what's best for you and contact an independent financial adviser, your bank or other financial institution for advice.

ENDOWMENT

An endowment plan consists of two elements: a savings scheme and a life assurance policy. The savings side puts money into a fund that is designed to pay off your mortgage. The life assurance element guarantees to pay a fixed amount if you die during the term of the plan. This fixed amount is usually equivalent to the value of the mortgage so if you die, the loan will be paid in full.

A few years ago, endowments were considered one of the best savings schemes next to interest only mortgages. But endowment plans do not always provide a large enough fund to pay the full cost of the mortgage. One of the reasons this has happened is that the rate at which the fund was expected to grow didn't achieve the growth targets expected by the industry. This is effected by a number of factors, including poor stock market performance.

The Financial Services Authority (FSA) is an independent, non-governmental body that has been given statutory powers under the Financial Services and Markets Act 2000. It regulates the financial services industry, including the insurance sector. It sets the industry standard growth rates that must be applied to any investment-related quotation, including endowment plans. A company can provide you with a quotation on a different rate to the FSAs, but it must be able to justify this fully to you and the FSA. The idea is that you always receive realistic quotations.

Despite the press about endowments, they could still be a viable option providing that the growth rate assumed at the start is achieved. It is important that you discuss this with an independent financial adviser.

INDIVIDUAL SAVINGS ACCOUNT AND PERSONAL EQUITY PLAN
This is one of the savings plans you might already invest in independent of your mortgage. The individual savings accounts (ISAs) and personal equity plans (PEPs) were introduced by the government to encourage people to invest in equities (companies listed on the stock exchange). Although your dividends can be reinvested in PEPs, you can no longer create or make further contributions to a PEP.

ISAs replaced PEPs and can be used as a way to save in order to achieve a lump sum to pay off your mortgage loan. Money saved through this scheme is free from capital gains and income tax. ISAs are flexible; you can cash in all or part of the fund at any time without penalty. The downside to these funds is that you have to make sure you don't raid the ISA piggy bank for today's needs at the expense of paying off your mortgage tomorrow.

The other issue with ISAs is that there is a limit to how much you can save each year. If you have an above average mortgage you may not be able to contribute enough each month to repay your mortgage.

PENSIONS
It is possible to take a part of your pension plan as a tax-free cash lump sum when you retire. Some plans even allow you to draw on your pension benefits without stopping work. Depending on how large your pension fund is, this sum could be used to repay all or part of your mortgage. The key benefit of using your pension scheme to help pay off your mortgage is that you get good tax benefits. Currently, as a basic rate taxpayer, for every £100 contributed to a pension plan you pay £78 and the

When you receive any investment-related quotation, make sure you also get a justification from the advisor. If quotes are significantly different from the ones recommended by the FSA, get the justification in writing and check it with an independent financial adviser.

government £22. If you were a higher rate taxpayer, you would only pay £60 for every £100.

As a result, you may be able to pay off your mortgage by making increased payments into your pension fund, providing it is achieving the expected growth rates. There are limits on the maximum contributions you can make, so you need to discuss this type of plan with your IFA or pension provider – be aware that unregulated mortgage advisors could not advise on this type of scheme. You will also only be able to pay off your mortgage once you draw the benefits from your pension.

INTEREST RATES

Apart from the two different types of mortgages and the different ways in which you can save to pay them, another variable to consider is the interest

IT'S UP TO YOU

If you want to be sure that your mortgage is paid off by the **end of the term date** (assuming you maintain your monthly mortgage payments), a repayment mortgage is an option to consider. But if you are prepared to accept a higher degree of risk, an interest only mortgage with a savings plan may be more attractive. You must always discuss this with a professional adviser.

You can use a **combination of savings schemes** to provide the lump sum needed to pay off the mortgage. Schemes can be optimised to give you greater financial flexibility and/or tax savings.

Everyone's circumstances are different. You should **seek professional advice** from an independent financial adviser or mortgage broker before making a decision.

INTEREST RATES

Because we pay our mortgage on a monthly basis for many years, it is difficult to realise how much you save by a small change in the level of interest rate you pay for your mortgage. This table shows an example of how much you would pay over the term of the mortgage if you borrowed £100,000. You can see that paying a lower interest rate can save you thousands of pounds over time and tens of thousands of pounds by paying off your mortgage faster.

Interest rate	Total paid to the mortgage lender over 15 years	Total paid to the mortgage lender over 25 years	Total paid to the mortgage lender over 30 years
4%	£133,000	£158,500	£172,000
4.2%	£135,500	£161,500	£176,000
4.6%	£138,500	£168,500	£184,500
6%	£152,000	£193,000	£216,000

rate. The interest rate is an extremely important variable to understand as even a small change can dramatically increase or decrease the amount you pay for your mortgage in the longer term. The rate affects the amount of money you have to repay every month. No matter what rate you choose or are offered, the type of mortgage you are buying does not change.

HOW LENDERS DECIDE TO LEND

Every mortgage lender has their own set of criteria to determine who they will lend to, how much and on what conditions. To apply for a mortgage, you will need to complete a mortgage application form. This consists of, among other things, your mortgage loan to value ratio, income and expenditure forecasts, employment status, credit history and details of the property type you want to purchase.

Loan to value is the amount of the mortgage expressed as a percentage of the property value. For example, if the property is worth £100,000 and you need a £90,000 mortgage then you have a loan to value ratio of 90%.

The more of your own cash you can use to buy a property, the more likely you are to obtain the mortgage you require, providing you meet other requirements. For example, if you have a higher deposit, the less you need to borrow and the less interest you pay. Some lenders offer more favourable interest rates if you have a low loan to value ratio.

Loan to value maximums could be 100% or even up to 130% of the property value. To get the better deals on mortgage rates, you would normally require 5–10% (or more) of the purchase price.

DIFFERENT TYPES OF INTEREST RATE

Standard variable: For a bank or building society to lend you money, they have to borrow themselves. They borrow from the Bank of England, which in turn charges them interest depending on the size of borrowing. The rate at which it charges them interest is called the **bank base rate (BBR)**. The Bank of England sets the rate at a monthly meeting.

The **standard variable rate (SVR)** is the base rate plus the profit a lender (the bank or building society) wants to make. So, for example, the base rate may be 4% with the lender charging you 2% above the base rate therefore equalling 6%. This is quoted as the SVR and it goes up and down at the lender's discretion. The lender may or may not decide to pass on changes in the base rate (up or down) to you through the SVR.

Fixed: The interest rate you repay on your mortgage is fixed for a period of time, for example two to five years. It doesn't matter during this time if the base or variable rate changes. Yours will be fixed at whatever rate you agreed for as long a period as you agreed. This is good if the rate rises, but bad if it falls. The main benefit is that you will know for a set amount of time exactly how much you will have to pay each month and can therefore plan your finances accordingly.

Discount rate: This rate is the SVR minus a discount that the lender gives. For example, if the SVR is 6% and you have a 1% discount, it will be 5%. As the SVR goes up or down, so does your final rate. The benefit is that you receive a reduction on the standard rate as well as reap benefits if the rate falls. Of course, the rate could go up, too.

Capped rate: A capped rate means you are getting a SVR, but the amount it can increase is finite – or capped – for a set period of time. For example, you may be on a SVR of 6% with a cap of 8% (top rate maximum). So if the rate increases dramatically during this time, then you benefit.

Tracker rate: This rate tracks the bank base rate. So you will usually be quoted a figure of BBR = 4% and your tracker rate will be 0.5% above this figure = 4.5%. Again, this is usually for a period of time, and means you benefit from any drops and keep saving if there are any increases, whatever the quoted SVR of the company is.

Do shop around on a regular basis – once or twice a year – to make sure you are on the best rate and take advantage of any new offers that come onto the market place. Be aware, however, that some mortgages carry a financial penalty if you move to a new lender within a certain time frame. If you do switch mortgages on the same property, you may be re-mortgaging and for this you may need a new survey to be undertaken (see page 119).

Lenders may, however, restrict your loan to value ratio depending on some other criteria.

Your ability to meet monthly payments is based on affordability. This is assessed by looking at the gross income of all parties contributing to the purchase plus details of actual expenditure over a given period. Don't

QUICK TIP **When buying a property with more than one person, it is better to check with your solicitor whether to use a beneficial joint tenancy or tenants in common agreement.**

forget that income is not just salary. It can also be regular profit from such things as investments, commissions, royalties or bonuses, for example. Some of the main expenditure items considered by a lender are listed on page 76. Expenditure are usually items such as existing mortgage/rent payments, bills, loans or hire purchase agreements, food, running costs of a car, clothes, maintenance or child support.

Be as accurate as you can when you give details of your expenditure. The mortgage lender will want to see evidence of both your income and expenditure. If you are not honest, this could affect your application.

EMPLOYMENT AND MORTGAGES

Many years ago, most of us were employed or self-employed. Contract and part-time work were not as popular as they are today. People are also more likely nowadays to go back to being a student and study half-way through their career. Your employment status may affect your ability to obtain a mortgage or limit the type of deal you can arrange. The riskier your employment position is perceived to be by the lender, the more difficult it will be to obtain a good deal.

If you are employed, you will need to prove this (a payslip or the P60 that you receive at the end of the tax year is usually enough). Sometimes a simple letter from your employer explaining your employment relationship (for example, if your salary is on a commission basis or you are part-time) will be sufficient.

Self-employed or those employed on a contract basis usually need to produce evidence of earnings – the last three years of your accounts or a letter from your accountant (or book keeper) will suffice.

Some companies will not lend to you if you do not have regular employment, even if you have the means to fund a mortgage (for

MAKING CONTACT To investigate the savings you can make by lowering the interest rate you pay or the time you take to pay off your mortgage, try visiting the following websites:
www.moneysupermarket.co.uk
www.charcolonline.co.uk
www.adviceonline.co.uk

example, you've saved up and are taking a year or more off for educational or other reasons). In this case you may need to find a specialist lender willing to accept your savings as proof that you can meet the payments. You can often do this through an independent financial advisor or by searching on the Internet.

Anyone who has ever borrowed money from a financial institution (including credit cards or owned a property) will have a credit history – a record of the value of any loans or extended payments you have obtained with a history of repayments. If you have ever failed to meet payments, you may be given an adverse report or lower credit rating. So, for example, if you've had a county court judgement (CCJ) or defaulted on a loan to the point that a court was involved, this may impact on your credit rating. Having an adverse credit rating or a CCJ doesn't stop you getting a mortgage, but it may limit who will lend to you and at what rate.

Not all lenders will lend on all properties. Some might restrict lending to properties of a certain age, properties that are freehold versus leasehold, particularly if the length of the leasehold is lower than the norm. Some lenders will lend for self-build properties and release mortgage monies bit by bit, whereas others may not lend on self-build at all.

Sometimes lenders place restrictions on loan to value ratio for certain property types. A good example of this is a converted property such as a house divided into two flats.

It may be worth the effort to keep a record of your personal circumstances and be ready to be open and honest about this history when you attempt to obtain a mortgage. Remember, too, that you will need to give a detailed description of the property you wish to buy before you make an offer or you could be rejected and lose the property as well as any money you have spent on legal and survey fees.

BEWARE OF HIDDEN COSTS

When applying for a mortgage there are a lot of hidden costs. If you already have a mortgage and want to change it – extend, borrow more or change the terms, for example – you may have to pay early redemption penalties. These usually depend on how long you have had the mortgage and the amount you pay each month. Typically you are charged a number of monthly mortgage payments (such as three or six months) as a penalty for redeeming the mortgage earlier than the agreed term. Some companies charge an administration fee for reserving funds for special mortgage deals such as fixed rate mortgages. The lender usually sends someone around to check the property or researches their databases to check the property is as you describe it.

Mortgage indemnity insurance is an insurance policy taken out to protect a mortgage with a typical loan to value ratio of 75% or more. Where the loan to value is up to 90%, the cost of the mortgage indemnity policy is often, but not always, absorbed by the lender. Where the loan to value exceeds this, the borrower would normally pay the premium via their lender. They will take this policy out on your behalf, but will charge you for it at the time of completion. It can cost thousands of pounds. If you default on your mortgage payment and the property is repossessed by the lender, the lender will sell the property. Any losses made on the mortgage to you are covered by the mortgage indemnity policy company. Be aware, however, that this company has the right to pursue you for the lost monies up to six years.

Some financial advisors and mortgage brokers also charge for their services. Fees are usually around 1% of the total value of the mortgage they arrange. While you may incur a cost, such advisors and brokers may

QUICK TIP Many people think the mortgage valuation approves the property's structure. It does not. It merely checks that the property exists and the description is accurate. You'll still need your own independent survey.

have special deals with financial institutions that can give you beneficial terms or interest rates or both. Always ask such advisors and brokers if any fees are involved or if their services are free to you and if the financial institution is paying them through some sort of commission or other arrangement. By law the company must quote this to you in a Terms of Business letter and on the financial statement you receive.

Finally, the deposit and mortgage money is usually transferred electronically and this is a banking service that you are charged for. Fees can vary considerably, so find out how much each transfer will be and if there are any ways to avoid multiple charges or to reduce the fees. With any mortgage deal, always ask what charges you will incur if you take out this mortgage and if there are any redemption penalties.

GETTING THE BEST DEALS

Getting the best deal could be something as simple as a different interest rate. But such details could save you considerable amounts over the lifetime of your mortgage. There are plenty of ways of finding the best deals. Nevertheless, only 50% of people change their mortgage lender when they move home. Many people also take out their buildings, contents, mortgage protection and life cover with the same lender even though they may be paying up to 40% more than if they went elsewhere.

Two good ways of finding the best mortgage and other finance deals are by researching on the Internet and using independent financial advice. There are hundreds of websites that try to gain your mortgage and financial business. The best ones to look out for are those that check lots of different lenders mortgages. You will need to be patient if you want to find the best deal on the web. For example, it can take up to 30 minutes to fill in some forms on-line.

MAKING CONTACT You can find an independent financial adviser at:
www.unbiased.co.uk

The best websites to use are those that offer independent financial advice rather than those that offer only their own mortgage schemes. After filling in their form, you will be given a list of possible mortgages to compare.

The key variables are the same as those outlined previously: mortgage type, interest rate, terms and monthly payments. Some sites also try to help you understand the true cost of the mortgage by assessing how much you would pay over a period of time. This helps you evaluate what may on the surface appear to be tempting – like cash back – but in the longer term may cost you more than another mortgage arrangement.

Some sites also give you the option to talk to someone rather than just filling in forms and receiving stock answers on-line. This can be helpful, particularly if you're not clear on the criteria or any terms and could help you avoid disappointment as well as rejection by a lender.

Although the Internet is great for research, unless you are a specialist you probably need someone who can advise you properly. A financial advisor will be able to discuss all your financial needs, looking at your circumstances and expectations as a whole and then suggest a financial plan or solution that gives you (as close as possible) what you want and need both now and in the future. If you don't have a financial advisor, talk to your bank, estate agent, solicitor or friends and family to ask if they can put you in touch with one. Alternatively, talk to your company as they may have special arrangements that may provide free advice.

RE-MORTGAGING

Re-mortgaging enables you to:

- Get a better deal on your mortgage
- Release money you need for something else, like to pay for property improvements.

If you are re-mortgaging, check other forms of financing, such as loans. They may be cheaper.

When re-mortgaging, the property will have to have a new mortgage valuation, more legals will be needed and your old mortgage redeemed. Each of these steps can incur **incremental cost** and you need to make sure you understand these implications and **check the benefit's true value.**

DEPOSITS

Unless you are buying a property with a 100% mortgage, you will need to ensure that you have enough money raised and ready at the time of exchange for the deposit. How much deposit you pay is usually dictated by three things: the loan to value ratio; the price of the property and what your legal representative agrees on your behalf.

Your deposit can come from one of several sources. If you have no property to sell, you will be expected to provide the funds in full yourself. Normally it takes five working days for the money to clear accounts.

If you are selling a property, whatever deposit you receive from your purchaser, it is then passed onto the person you are buying from. However, if the deposit required is more than you are receiving from your sale, you need to provide the balance of funds to your legal representative.

Although there is an average amount usually recommended for deposit, the final decision is between you, your purchaser and the person from whom you are buying. It can be anything as long as you all agree and have your money ready in time.

INSURANCE **NEEDS**

Normally when you apply for a mortgage, your lender will also send you quotes and information about other financial packages including insurance. Check out the competition. You may be able to get a better deal elsewhere. Compare quotes to make sure that you are getting a good deal as insurance can be expensive. Sticking with your current insurer may not necessarily give you a better deal. So, whatever deals come your way, check them out, it could save you hundreds of pounds.

Remember, your building insurance must be in place at the time of exchange as you become legally responsible for the property's insurance as soon as you exchange contracts. Contents insurance should stop in your current home (if you have one) on the day you move out and, if required, begin immediately in the new one the day you move in.

How much you should insure the building for is usually something your surveyor can estimate. Double-check this valuation with your mortgage lender. The cover is always less than the actual price you pay for the property as you are insuring the rebuild of the property to its current layout and condition. When you buy a property you also buy the land and space it occupies. This is what makes the difference in value.

It is imperative that you have organised your buildings insurance BEFORE you exchange contracts on your new purchase. Not only that but you need to ensure that your solicitor has a copy of the policy and the policy number so that this can be given to the lender (to reassure them that they can send the monies out) and the seller so they are aware that the property continues to be insured between exchange and completion.

When asking for a quote, see if the company pays to house you while your property is being rebuilt or if you have any say in the rebuild and the excess amount you may have to pay.

QUICK TIP **Many companies give information on what is not covered. It is important that you check this in detail and think through the various circumstances and scenarios you can imagine and see if these are covered by the policy.**

As with mortgages and insurance, you do not need to take out your buildings and contents insurance with the same company, but many people do and you often will get a discount as a result. Contents insurance covers the items in your home. It's not difficult to get competitive quotes, but you need to understand the differences between them. Check what's included and what isn't. For example, some cover cash losses, others don't; some replace goods at the same price you paid while others take into account the cost of brand new items. The excess you pay – what you agree to pay before you ask the insurer to start paying – is another variable. Some policies cover goods and cash outside the house, say when you are travelling or on holiday.

Whatever insurance you go for, again check out exactly what is not covered. For example, if you have a business laptop or work from home, this equipment may need to be covered separately.

PERSONAL INSURANCE PLANS

As buying a property is probably one of the biggest financial commitments you'll make, it's important you protect this asset the best way you can. You can do this through:

- Life assurance.
- Critical illness cover.
- Permanent health insurance.
- Accident sickness and unemployment cover.

Legally you don't have to take out any of these, but **life assurance may be compulsory** depending on your circumstances and your lender's conditions.

LIFE ASSURANCE

There are many different types of assurance but the main one that effects your property purchase are level term assurance and decreasing term assurance (the latter is mortgage protection cover). The reason you should consider taking this out is that it ensures that if you die, your mortgage will be repaid in full, protecting you, your family or any other dependents.

A level term assurance policy is a plan that runs for a set period of time (usually the same length as your mortgage term), and will pay out a fixed amount (usually the same as your mortgage), on your death. The money typically goes to your estate and can be used to pay off the mortgage. This type of policy often works with an interest only mortgage (see page 100) as the amount of your loan and life cover would stay constant throughout the term you borrow. If you survive this term then the policy will cease and will be worthless.

Decreasing term assurance (or mortgage protection cover) works in a similar way to level term, but the amount of payment reduces throughout your mortgage term. For example if you have £100,000 worth of cover, and you die in year 1 this is the sum that is likely to need repaying and they will do so. By year 15 the amount will be a lot less as much of the mortgage will have been paid off. This is most suited to a repayment mortgage as your original mortgage amount is reduced each year. The monthly premiums for this policy are therefore typically cheaper than level term.

CRITICAL ILLNESS COVER

This type of policy will pay out on the diagnosis of a stated critical illness that is likely to impact on your ability to earn and pay your mortgage. It is only the diagnosis that is required, so would be in addition to the Life Assurance cover you take out. The amount that is paid out is a lump sum, usually equivalent to the value of the mortgage.

This type of policy can be taken out for either repayment or interest only mortgages.

PERMANENT HEALTH INSURANCE

This pays out a regular income (usually monthly) in case you cannot do your job due to a medical problem, enabling you to continue to make your mortgage repayments while you recuperate or for as long as it takes to pay off the mortgage.

This type of policy can be taken out with either mortgage type and can be in addition to critical illness as both policies cover different medical conditions.

ACCIDENT, SICKNESS AND UNEMPLOYMENT

This policy pays out a regular income in case of accidents, some forms of sickness and if you become unemployed. However, it only covers your mortgage payments so is not as comprehensive as the permanent health insurance, but has the added benefit of protecting your payments from redundancy.

An ideal scenario is to have life, critical and permanent health insurance. But before taking out these insurances you should check whether you get any of these types of cover via other plans or via your employee benefits packages.

AFTER THE RESEARCH COMES **THE OFFER**

Once you have decided to make an offer on the property, you need to decide what is the minimum and maximum you think you can offer. Setting limits is a good way to buy with your head, not heart, especially if you get into a bidding war.

There are various ways of making an offer. Normally it is done via the agent, but there is no harm in trying to negotiate with the vendor yourself – particularly if they are happy to do this. It just depends on how happy you and the vendor are to negotiate and sort out things if anything goes wrong.

When making your offer, it is helpful to all parties to explain why you are making it and what conditions you may wish to attach. For example, you may be making an offer under the asking price because you can't afford to pay more or you really think the property's not worth more. If your offer is rejected, it will be easier to explain if you've made it clear why you made the offer you have. You may be offering a lower price because you feel there is a lot of work needed on the property and have taken this into consideration. Maybe you think there are other properties that are priced better and that you genuinely believe the property is overpriced.

Whatever your reasons, justify them. You want to avoid the vendor feeling you are making an insulting offer.

WHEN, WHAT AND HOW TO MAKE AN OFFER

Making an offer on a property can be a tricky decision. If you have got to this stage, you have probably seen a lot of properties and rejected most of them for some reason. Now you've found just the right one, so it's time to think how you want to make the offer.

If you make your offer and you're accepted immediately, you may have offered too much. If you make too low an offer, you might be rejected

QUICK TIP Always find out why a property hasn't sold if it's been on the market for a while. If the reason is something you cannot easily rectify, you may find the property equally hard to sell when you're ready to move on.

and not given another chance. Your offer may spark a bidding war and you could end up losing the property.

As the buyer, you know exactly what you can afford and what you're willing to pay. So remember you are working from a position of strength, not weakness.

The first question to ask yourself is if the property is giving you good value for the money. What is it about this property that makes it good value (the road it's on, what it backs onto, or is it that the estate agent and seller are pricing the property more realistically than others)?

If the property has just come onto the market, you may want to wait for a few weeks to see if anyone else makes an offer first or you may want to snap it up before anyone else has the chance to make an offer. If you make the offer, try to have the property taken off the market immediately with a 'Sale Agreed' or 'Sold Subject to Contract' on the sale board. The agent may not be able to do this for you unless you agree to pay a premium or can guarantee a certain completion date.

If the property has been on the market for more than six months, you need to know why. Has a sale fallen through and, if so, for what reasons? What's the feedback from other viewers?

How quickly does the seller want to move? If they are not bothered, they may be less likely to accept an offer. However, if they have found a house and can't progress that purchase until they have an offer or have another compelling reason, they may be more likely to accept an offer. That's why you need to know as much about their circumstances as you can.

What can the agent tell you? The agent's job is to get the best price they can (remember they usually only get paid on completion). It is also a legal requirement that the agent passes on any offers received, no matter how low. Discuss with the agent what type of offer the sellers want. You

Agents are not allowed to tell you what offers other people make. They can, however, steer you towards a price if you ask for their advice.

may even be able to bounce some figures around with them to gauge reaction.

While it is in the agent's interest to get the best price, they also want a serious offer that's able to progress successfully to completion and so may help you get your offer accepted.

KEEP YOUR OPTIONS OPEN

If you have several properties you like, you are in a good negotiating position. You can offer exactly what you are happy to pay. If your first choice is rejected, you have a fallback position. But if you have been hunting for a while and this is the only property you have seen that fits your needs, you may want to think things through carefully and make an offer the seller can't (or at least is unlikely to) refuse.

BIDDING WARS

If more than one offer is on the table, some agents will suggest that all parties make their final offers in writing. The highest bidder or the person in the best position to complete the purchase is then likely to be chosen.

Don't get involved in a bidding war unless you really want the property. Once you're involved in a bidding war, there is no point worrying about the other parties. Remember, even if you lose, the sale may fall through and you might have another chance. But don't get your hopes up too high.

If you are a cash buyer, you'll be in a strong position. If you have a property to sell, be clear about what stage your sale is at. The further along you are, the more likely you will be top of the list to be chosen.

Even after you have made an offer and it is accepted – or if you have lost to another party – nothing's final until the property has been surveyed and the legal side has been completed. Things may change.

MAKING CONTACT

Royal Institute of Chartered Surveyors (RICS)
Tel: **0870 333 1600**
Website: **www.ricsfirms.co.uk**

Allied Surveyors
Tel: **08700 740750**
Website: **www.alliedsurveyors.com**

On average in the UK, one in three sales fall through after offer stage, because of problems with the survey reports or because the local searches have thrown up issues such as flooding or changes to the area that may adversely effect the property's price. So, once an offer is made, be prepared to understand that there may be issues you do not yet know about, which may result in you pulling out of the sale or reducing your offer price.

SURVEYING THE PROPERTY

A survey on the property is needed after you have made an offer. This will also help you decide whether or not to go ahead with the purchase. An independent survey checks that the price you have agreed is reasonable. It will also highlight any problems that might need correcting before or after you move in. A professional surveyor who has a specialist degree and is a member of the Royal Institute of Chartered Surveyors (RICS) carries out property surveys in the UK.

Buying a home without a survey can be dangerous. Nevertheless, only 20–25% of people have a survey done. In this section the three different levels of report/survey are described together with information on why you need one, how to choose one and how to best interpret the report to assess whether you should go ahead with the purchase.

Remember, the estate agent is not qualified to take the property's physical condition into consideration when suggesting a price. Their price is always subject to survey. So you as a buyer make an offer based on what you can see. A survey, on the other hand, will be able to spot things like damp, necessary roof repairs, rotting timber and other structural defects such as subsidence. Correcting some defects can be costly, so you need to know what to expect.

You can find a surveyor through an estate agent, your lender or your legal representative. RICS keeps a register of member surveyors (see Making contact, page 119). Ideally, get a recommendation from a friend or someone who has recently moved and was happy with their surveyor.

ORGANISING AND CHOOSING A SURVEYOR

Once your offer has been accepted, appoint a surveyor to carry out an HSV or a building survey. Get two or three quotes from recommended companies. Also ask them about their experience and knowledge in the area you are buying, what type of survey they would recommend, how long it would take and when they could have the report to you. Also check if you can discuss the report with them once you have studied it.

DIFFERENT TYPES OF SURVEYS

A mortgage valuation is the cheapest way to value a property and many buyers believe it also covers them for any defects. However, it is commissioned not by you, but by your lender – even though you pay for it. Its purpose is to reassure the lender that the property is valued correctly and won't really look at much else. They need this so that if you fail to meet your mortgage payments and repossess the property, they can recover their costs when selling it. It is not a survey.

A homebuyer survey and valuation (HSV) is a standard report developed by RICS and used by surveyors to evaluate any urgent repairs required. For example, rising damp or potential defects that require further investigation such as checking the condition of a flat roof. The report should also highlight any maintenance and other things that you should be aware of like the need to replace windows within a certain number of years to noise from a busy road that might affect a future sale.

A buildings survey (also called structural survey) is the most comprehensive type. The surveyor will provide a detailed report on the property's construction and major and minor defects. It is a more in-depth version of the HSV and is suitable for old or listed buildings, properties that have been altered or you intend to alter, or an unusual property. Although this report does not include a valuation, one can be provided on request.

QUICK TIP

For leasehold properties, the freeholder pays for the building cover and you pay part of this cost; a surveyor will look for some confirmation of this for their report.

Don't ignore the surveyor's recommendations for further investigation for damp, timber rot, roofing or utility issues. These are costly to put right. Now is the time to renegotiate the property offer to take such costs into account.

Your lender may offer you a reduced-cost survey if you book through them. Check how many surveyors are on their panel and how many surveys they do every day as well as if they are local. Don't just accept the offer; compare it with other local surveyors to make sure you are obtaining a good deal and a fully qualified surveyor who will spend time on the property you want to buy.

Your chosen surveyor should recommend which survey to have. For standard properties built after the 1900s and not undergone any major alterations, the HSV may be enough. This type of survey takes several hours and the surveyor will need to liaise with the selling agent or the vendor to organise access to the property.

A surveyor will be worried about missing something that later needs rectifying and the possibility they may be sued for this oversight. Many properties have fitted carpets so flooring may be difficult to check in detail. The surveyor may not be able to assess the potential damage from underground defects that cannot be seen. Surveys come with their own set of terms and conditions so make sure you read these carefully before you instruct a surveyor. One company, Allied Surveyors (see Making contact, page 119), offers an insurance policy as part of its surveying packages, which will cover you if 'hidden defects' are found. Others may, too.

WHAT SURVEYS COVER

An HSV or buildings survey will recommend any urgent, necessary or possible actions that you may need to take and cover:

- Type and age of the property
- Property construction, inside and out
- Confirmation of the rooms on the sales particulars and any exterior buildings or grounds

QUICK TIP   If you know that access to certain parts of the property will be required, make sure that you let the surveyor know so they can ensure they have access on the day. Put this in writing so you have comeback if required.

- Location description
- Highlight potential structural defects requiring further investigation
- Check timber and insulation and for damp and condensation
- Check access to utility services highlighting if further investigation is needed as well as where stopcocks, tanks and meters are located
- Provide notes for your legal representative

Surveys do not cover anything that the surveyor cannot access at the time of their visit or that is hidden, such as under carpeted floors.

REPORT, REVIEW AND ACTION!

After you receive your survey report, take time to read it thoroughly. Make notes on anything you do not understand or on any suggestions the survey makes, highlighting whatever needs repairing or investigating. Then contact your surveyor to answer your questions and obtain an estimate of how much it may cost to fix or investigate anything they have mentioned. Decide if you are happy with the valuation. If you are now aware of work that needs doing, you may want to reduce your offer to account for the additional cost and inconvenience it causes. You may prefer the vendor does this before you exchange or complete contracts.

Your lender may only agree to release part of the mortgage funding when essential work is done. In any of these circumstances, make sure you are clear about why you are reducing your offer and give evidence to support your decision, if you can, as this will help the vendor to understand (and hopefully more readily accept) your new price.

Don't forget to send a copy of the report to your legal advisor in case there is information in the survey that impacts on the transfer of the title. For example, comments on an extension might result in a request for planning permission documents from the seller.

CONVEYANCING

The legal process required to transfer the ownership of the property and agreed fixtures and fittings to your name is called 'buying legals'. The legal term for property transfer is conveyancing. How to choose a company and the different types of services that are offered for both these services have already been described (see page 40).

Understanding the legal process as a buyer is essential if you want to remain in control. From the buyer's perspective the legal processes are more involved than selling and the company you work with needs to liaise between the vendor's solicitor, your mortgage company, the local council, Land Registry and sometimes even the surveyor. A key part of your legal representative's role is ensuring that nothing is happening in the area that will impact on the price or the land value now and in the future. This includes planning permission applications already lodged for such things as new transport, building projects, environmental issues or other things that may affect your purchase. This is just one reason why the legal costs when you buy are usually more than when you sell.

Your legal representative should guide you on any purchase issues such as checking buying terms for the building, the land and any fixtures and fittings.

WHO, WHAT AND WHEN

When you buy, you cannot formally instruct a legal representative until you have found a property to purchase. All of the work will be associated with a particular property and your mortgage offer, so there is nothing that can be done before you make an offer. But you can choose a legal representative before you make an offer and this might help speed things up. In fact, this is a good move as many estate agents will not accept an offer until you have the details of your legal company available.

Try to agree a 'no sale, no fee' option with your representative (see page 42). When buying, this is a good option as there is potentially unlimited work required, resulting in a higher price than the original quote. For example, you might find additional research is required to find planning permission documents for an extension. With fixed fee conveyancing this would be included in the price. It is helpful, too, if you have spent money on a survey and as a result decide to pull out from the purchase. At least you won't have to incur wasted solicitor's charges too.

Having chosen a legal representative, once your offer has been verbally accepted, the estate agent will write to you and the vendor giving details in the letter of both the legal representatives and confirming the offer price. This usually takes place within 48 hours of your offer being accepted, but you can advise your legal representative immediately, tell them of the letter, give them the address of the property and discuss the timeframe that it will take to complete: usually between six and 12 weeks.

HOW LONG SHOULD IT TAKE?

The whole process is quite complex. From a buyer's perspective – and your legal representative's – you are at the mercy of everyone else doing what you need them to do. Your legal contact asks, chases and analyses the information and prepares a report on all the legal aspects of your purchase and mortgage that could have an impact on your purchase. But to write the report, the legal representative has to wait for paperwork from the vendor (and their legal representative), the local council, the Land Registry and the mortgage lender, as well as liaise with the banks.

To ensure all this happens as quickly as possible use a company that really understands the process. Talk to your legal representative at the beginning so you know what issues are likely to come up and agree what, when and how you will be updated. Also talk about what you can do to help. For example, local searches can take up to six weeks although some

QUICK TIP The same legal company cannot work for both the buyer and the seller. If the seller's representative has already started the legal work, you'll have to choose a different one.

councils let you to do this on-line, which can be quicker. Your mortgage application could take weeks or months and the vendor's representative might take six weeks or more to apply for their client's title deeds and document and then prepare the contract and send the forms over to your legal representative. Hopefully though, your vendor will have already started this process when the house was put up for sale. As long as you know what is holding up the process, you and your legal contact can work together to try to put the necessary pressure on the party that is stopping movement.

Ensure you send the paperwork back as quickly as possible after checking it carefully. Send your money for exchange and completion in good time. You can deliver papers by hand or use next day delivery services, preferably ones with some tracking ability and insurance, just in case. If everyone involved in the process did this, it could shave weeks off your purchase time.

CONVEYANCING FINANCIALS

When you receive information from your legal representative, you should also get a statement that explains what money has come and gone from the account held on your behalf. So you can check this, overleaf on page 127 is an explanation of what the legal terms mean. At the end of the process, your legal representative will invoice you if they are owed anything (this is usually just their fee) or refund any excess minus what they are owed.

SELF-CONVEYANCING

Much of the work described on these pages is simply a case of requesting, collecting and chasing information from other parties. By doing it yourself you can **save several hundreds of pounds.**

However, you may find your mortgage lender will stipulate in your agreement with them that you appoint a licensed conveyancer or solicitor. Your lender needs to protect its money and rights to sell the property if you default on your loan.

If you go down the self-conveyancing route, then it is a good idea to get **some legal advice** once you have all of the information you need on the contents, especially the title, search forms and contract from the buyer. This stage needs **exceptional attention to detail** and specialist knowledge to understand – not just a quick look from you.

CHAINS – AND HOW TO
DEAL WITH THEM

When buying and selling a property there is always a party at the beginning and end. For example, a first-time buyer, their seller who may be buying another property, the vendor of that second property who may be buying a brand new home or moving abroad. Chains can be made of two or more parties. The average in England and Wales is seven.

One of the main frustrations for all is the number of people that need to be liaised with and relied on to do their job well. An average exchange could involve seven different selling agents working with eight different legal companies – all trying to collect, swap and confirm information to exchange or complete across the chain on the same day.

As your purchase (and sale) relies on so many other parties, the better the relationship you have with the companies working for you and the better you understand the length of the chain and the parties involved, the more reassurance you may have that the chain will not break.

It is hard to manage chains. Ideally, there would be one person in charge of the whole chain. But this just doesn't happen. Legal companies can't act for buyers and sellers of the same property. Estate agents can only manage the sale of the property and can't organise the finances that lead to the purchase. As a result you can only try to obtain answers to key questions up and down the chain as soon as possible and encourage everyone involved to give the answers back. Whatever happens, when you are involved in a chain, the whole process can only move as fast as the slowest sale or purchase.

If you are involved in a chain, the first thing to understand is who is buying and selling from who, and ask your estate agent to tell you how many people/properties are in the chain. Gain some reassurance that they all have sold offers and no one is waiting for a buyer. Ideally, you want to know who are cash buyers and who – both below and above you in the

FIVE REASONS WHY CHAINS BREAK

1 A buyer offers more than they can afford and their mortgage application fails.

2 An adverse survey results in a buyer pulling out.

3 A seller withdraws due to change of circumstance.

4 Problems with the property title or planning causes a buyer to withdraw.

5 Timetable changes or delays cause a buyer or seller to withdraw.

chain – are relying on mortgage offers and whether they have been applied for.

You can also do things yourself to make the process shorter. For example, if your buyer can proceed quickly, go ahead if you can. If you can't move into your property at the same time, arrange for temporary accommodation and put your goods in storage. So if your purchase falls through, you are now in an excellent position to proceed on another property as a cash buyer.

If you are buying a new home, find out if the building company are willing to offer a part-exchange scheme, in case your buyer pulls out. With these schemes you may not achieve the sale price you want, but you don't have to pay estate agent fees and money can be transferred quickly.

AVOIDING CHAINS ALTOGETHER

Try to avoid chains of more than four parties. You can even avoid chains altogether by:

- Selling to cash buyers – first time buyers, renters or investors
- Opting for a part-exchange scheme
- Moving to temporary accommodation, then looking for a new home
- Buying a newly built home
- Buying an already vacated home

Of course, these options limit your range of potential properties to purchase.

BUYING A PROPERTY IN **SCOTLAND**

When you are dealing with a property centre who handles both the marketing and the legal side, do not change the way you work with them. It is still the same as working with an estate agent and legal representative.

This is a different system to England and Wales. In some ways it is better, but this is mainly from the seller's and the successful buyer's perspective. For unsuccessful buyers it can be costly and frustrating. In this section the main differences are highlighted together with advice on how to keep the costs down and tips on how to cope when things go wrong.

House hunting in Scotland is similar to England and Wales. Choose an area and a road where you'd like to live. The main difference is that property centres as well as estate agents market and sell the properties. They handle both the marketing and the legal side for the vendor, which can be helpful in that you're dealing with one less company.

MAKING AN OFFER

Two differences when looking at properties are that the prices you see are not asking prices and that you have to register an interest if you are thinking of buying. The prices that properties are advertised for are only guidelines. Typically they are 10% below what the bid price and final price is likely to be. It is important to remember this as it can make a big difference to what you can and can't afford, how you brief the property centres and whether you will be able to make a successful bid or not.

If you visit a property you like and think you might like to make an offer, you need to register your interest. You can do this over the phone, but preferably in writing, via your legal company, to the property centre/ selling agent. When you make an offer you send a written bid price together with details of your circumstances. These may include proposed completion dates and any clauses to the purchase such as fixtures and fittings you want included or to make an offer on, as well as whether you are a cash buyer or still have to sell your property. Bids must be received within a deadline. By registering your interest you are kept in the loop.

EASING THE COST OF SEVERAL SURVEYS

Fortunately, over the last few years a new system has been developed to help everyone who wants to make an offer.

● A company (such as Surveys on Line at www.surveysonline.co.uk) organises with the vendor for a survey to be done on their property. It is done initially at no charge to the vendor and is made available on-line.

● Buyers can then purchase the survey at a price lower than if it had been organised individually. The potential buyers can check the condition of the property and the party that makes the successful bid then pays the balance of the cost of the survey. If the property is withdrawn from sale, the vendor picks up the tab.

Ask the property centre about companies that run this type of service and for lists of properties that have this facility.

In England and Wales you do this when the offer has been accepted. In Scotland you do this, along with other interested parties, before you know if you will be successful in purchasing the property. You may end up paying for several surveys before securing a property. To combat this, some agents now accept offers 'subject to survey'. The timeframe to get the survey, however, is short – often 24 hours.

When you send in your bid, the property centre will be looking for two things. The main one is the best offer and completion date. But it will also be looking for the party in the best position to purchase. For example, your bid might not be the highest, but you might be best placed to proceed immediately with the purchase.

WHAT HAPPENS ON THE BID DAY

On bid day, at the appointed time, all the bids are opened and reviewed. The property centre contacts and discusses the bids with the vendor and one party is chosen. Everyone who has placed a bid is then notified. At that point you can ask why you weren't successful and seek advice on what you should do next time. If you are successful, the rest of the process is similar to completing in England and Wales.

TROUBLE SHOOTING

When looking for a property	**What's your problem?**	**Who can help you?**
	The estate agent does not send you sales particulars	Estate agent concerned (see page 15)
	You can't find a property you like	Estate agents Personal research Buying agent
Once you have made your offer	An offer made is rejected	Estate agent

What can be done?

- Ring or call in to talk to the agent. Check they have your details on file and that these are correct. Also ask if the brief you have given is feasible and that this agent does secure the type of property and the price range that you are looking at.

- Ask how often they update their website. If every 24 hours, then it may be as well to check this daily or sign up to text and email updates. Nearly all of the sales particulars are on these sites so you can even print them for yourself.

- Do not forget to look at the local property paper weekly, too, as most new listings are advertised within the first two weeks.

- Check first that what you have briefed for exists in the areas you are looking in. Then double-check that they are within your price range. If you see houses you like but none are for sale, talk to the agent and ask when was the last time these properties came up for sale and if they have valued any recently.

- If you really like a road or property, put a polite note through the door with your contact details, you never know. Alternatively, ask your agent to help you with this.

- You may need to adjust your price range or the area radius you are looking at to get what you want, or you may need to change your brief to one that covers more properties for sale.

- Another solution might be to talk to a local builder and see if they have any plans for the type of property you are looking for or could help you even build your own.

- Try to ensure you get a reason why it has been rejected. Have they had similar or higher offers already? Is it your own circumstances – have you not sold yet?

- If the offer is rejected now, will the vendors consider it in the future?

- Ask the agent too if they will let you know if any other offers come forward so you have an opportunity to increase your own offer if that is the issue. You can increase the offer if it helps, but insist the property is withdrawn from the market.

	What's your problem?	**Who can help you?**
	You have made an offer, which has been accepted, but the agent/vendor will not take the property off the market	Estate agent (see page 15) Legal company (see page 40)
	The property is unexpectedly withdrawn from the market	Estate agent (see page 15) Legal company (see page 40)
	One of the legal companies does not appear to be progressing the sale or the paperwork	Legal company (see page 40) Selling estate agent (see page 15)
	Someone else makes a higher offer	Estate agent (see page 15) Legal company (see page 40)
Once you have reached exchange/completion	Exchange/completion does not happen on the day planned	Legal company (see page 40) Estate agent (see page 15)
	Problems with money transfer on completion day	Legal company (see page 40)

What can be done?

- Unfortunately, this is probably right as 1:3 sales fall through after offer stage. What you can do is to raise your offer to try and have it taken off the market.
- You could ensure you are told of other offers if they come through before the vendor chooses someone else or that if any other offers do come through, then sealed bids are made.
- If the survey and mortgage application have already gone through, you may ask for them to withdraw it then as at this stage you are more likely to be able to complete on the purchase.
- Talk to your legal contact to see if they can suggest anything else that can be done, such as an interim agreement. It may cost a little more, but this could save time and hassle later on.

- You need to understand why. It may be a temporary or permanent situation. Ask if there is anything that can be done to continue with the purchase – even if it means exchanging now and completing later down the line.
- You could try to gain an agreement that you have first refusal if it does come back onto the market. Your legal company should help you with this.

- To deal with this effectively, you need to ask the right questions to know what is not happening and what can be done to speed things up. For example, if you haven't received confirmation that the searches have been done, ask when they were applied for and when they are expected. Offer to chase the council if necessary.
- If it is the vendor's legal company that is not sending information over, ring the estate agent and ask them to ask the buyers to chase them; it might even be that the vendors have not filled the form in.
- At least if the right questions are being asked and everyone is communicating once or twice a week, then the work should move forward. If nothing changes, then one party can consider switching legal companies.

- Check if this has been accepted yet and consider whether you want to make a higher one or if matching the rival offer would be enough.
- Talk to your legal company to gain confirmation that the offer has been made. Ask the status of the rival bidder – are they cash buyers or do they have a property to sell?
- If this does happen, start looking for another property too, just so that you keep your options open if it happens again. The sale may still fall through and, if so, you would be in a strong position to re-negotiate.

- Find out via your legal company why it has not gone through. Is someone else holding things up further down the line? Can this be avoided next time? Have you sent the necessary monies and are these cleared in your legal company's account?

- This is down to the legal companies, the lender and the banks to sort. On one day you can only have so many bank transfers as there is a limit with opening and closing time and how long the money takes to get from lender to legal account to vendor's legal account up the chain. Two sets of money transfers should be feasible.
- If you are higher up the chain, any more than that and you may need to consider staying somewhere overnight just in case you need an extra day for funds to clear.

SECTION THREE

MOVING
HOME

You've reached exchange and the day of completion is in sight –
now is the time to get your house sorting and packing underway.
This chapter begins with how to find and choose a reputable
remover; we outline the pros and cons of using professionals or
doing it yourself. The count down to the Big Day is filled with
important things to do – follow this chapter and you won't miss
out on any of them. Then once you are settled in your new home
you will want to make it your own, which is easily done if you
follow the guidance on these pages.

BRITISH ASSOCIATION OF REMOVERS

BAR is an association funded by its members. Each member has to have an inspection before joining. This inspection reviews facilities and vehicles, financial record keeping, trained staff and internal procedures. Members can be checked **at any time** after joining.

The association likes all of its members to achieve the **Quality Standard for Household Moving** – BS EN 12522 – a standard that is recognised across both Britain and Europe.

CHOOSING A REMOVAL COMPANY

When considering which company to use, start from the moment you first contact them. Do they answer the phone promptly and sound like they are interested in your business? Are they helpful and efficient in organising a quote for you? Have they made an effort to give you useful information to help you move or a website you can use as well as various ways to contact them (email, telephone). Were they on time for their visit to your property? Did they have a thorough look at your property and its contents? If it took only a few minutes, I would worry that the quote may not be accurate.

When showing them around, show them everywhere. A good company will make sure you do and will also ask a lot of questions about what is going and what might be staying. Fully brief the company. If you don't, you could find that they may refuse to move specific items on the day, or charge much more that the original quote. Worse still, the vehicle may not be big enough to take everything.

Some of the items people forget about are those already in storage or with friends/family. Don't forget the loft, spare room, garage, sheds or anywhere you may have put things you don't often use. If you are taking a shed, greenhouse or other large item with you to the new property, check this is included in the quote.

It's also important to understand the employment policy of the removal companies you short list. Because it's a cyclical business, try to avoid temporary staff and inexperienced people moving your personal property. Ask about the average length of time their removal staff have been working for them. Ask what percentage of clients have complained about their services over the last six months or year and enquire about how complaints are managed. You could also ask for local references.

WHEN DO PEOPLE MOVE?

One of the biggest problems for removal companies is that moving home is not just seasonal but heavily weighted **to the end of a month** and usually a Friday. Their busiest time is the summer months (June to August) and often near bank holidays. So if you plan to move at this time, you need to give as much notice as possible to removal companies. The British Association of Removers and all reputable removal companies recommend **you move on any day except Friday**, particularly during busy months. Many will offer or negotiate a discount if you choose another day.

The main benefit to you of moving early during the week is that if there are problems on the day of the move, the company and the vehicle is more likely to be able to help you by **staying later or keeping your items in the vehicle overnight** as they are less likely to have to empty and clean the vehicle for use the next day. If you move on a Friday and something goes wrong, you probably won't be able to get help until the Monday and may incur charges for the items kept in storage over the weekend.

The main organisation of your removals can be done at any time if you are selling a property. Most removal companies expect you to be close to exchange before you contact them for a quote. Remember, once you have accepted or made an offer on a property, you need to contact your short list of removers **three to four weeks before the day** or week you hope to move. This gives all the companies time to look around the property, send you a quote and organise the date for moving. You need to book the exact day with the removal company at least two weeks before the actual moving day.

Not all companies will come and quote for your removals. With the Internet, some have websites where you can complete a form giving details of your property and its belongings. These companies use averages to calculate how much your move will be. If you use this method, make sure you print the form first. Use this as a checklist, going around each room of your house to make sure that you fill in the form accurately.

However you get your quotes, if you have an unusual situation, make sure the removal company knows. For example, if there is restricted access, a narrow lane, a one-way street or security approval needed for a gated community or private road, the removal company needs to know in advance. It may need to use two vans rather than one large vehicle. It will also need to know of any unusual items you want to move, such as a greenhouse, shed or just lots of plants or flowers.

If you are unsure, then ask the removal company to come and visit the premises to confirm their quote. This will save you – and the removers – any unwanted hassle on the day or surprise surcharges at the end of your move.

During their visit, they should also take time to talk you through all the different services they offer. The main ones are packing, storage and to fill it. Use this figure, too, when talking to the vehicle rental companies. They can advise you on the size of vehicle you will need.

HIRING A VEHICLE FOR YOUR MOVE

On your standard driving licence, you can drive vehicles up to and including a 7.5 ton Gross Vehicle Weight (GVW). Anything bigger and you would need to have the relevant Heavy Goods Vehicle licence. Always check with your car insurance which vehicles you are covered to drive and your household insurance what will and won't be covered.

Once you've decided on what vehicle to use, get quotes from different rental companies. If you are moving locally, look at both local and national companies. However, if you are moving some distance, you may need to book through a national company as it will be easier to drop off the vehicle to a local depot rather than return it to where you hired it. Vehicle hire companies are usually listed in local telephone directories and newspapers. Your estate agent may be also be able to recommend one.

Rental companies normally require a deposit in case there is any damage to the vehicle or you return it late. Deposits can be up to several hundred pounds. Many hire companies will also offer you the option to buy additional insurance. Before you sign for this, check the costs of additional cover with your own insurance company. Finally, some companies have restrictions on renting depending on your age, so check what you can and cannot have prior to deciding to move yourself.

PACKING YOUR LIFE AWAY

Whether moving yourself or with professional help, you may decide to pack everything yourself. Some removal firms will drop off packing material in advance to enable you to do this but if you need to find

QUICK TIP
Wrap valuable and fragile items carefully in protective wrapping such as bubble wrap and clearly mark the box as fragile. You may want to use a colour coding system so you (and the removal company) know which boxes may be stacked and which need to be treated with the greatest care.

packing material, ask at local shops for boxes. You can also ask local storage companies for boxes and packing material. Alternatively, buy the boxes, packing material and crates that you will need. Although this may be expensive, you'll have similar sized boxes that maybe easier to stack, load and unload. If you have items that are valuable or fragile, you might prefer to use specialist boxes and tea chests that are used for antiques. Companies such as www.a1box.co.uk or local removal companies should be able to help you.

Clearly mark all boxes and items with which floor and room they are going into. For example, bedroom one furniture in your old property may be moving to bedroom two in the new property. At both properties label each room so that it is clear where each item and box it to be moved to.

If you decide to pack yourself, do this as far in advance of the actual moving day as possible. Work out what you can pack early and what has to wait until more or less the last minute. List the items that you need and will be packing away on a count-down to moving day schedule, for example, what can be packed one, two or three weeks before the move. Consider the time of year. If it's winter, garden furniture, tools and summer clothes may already be packed away. Items such as ornaments, books, CDs and anything in the loft can be packed early, too.

If you have items in storage, make sure these are moved from your old home or picked up from storage and taken to the new property.

Also, start an 'eat everything in the cupboards and freezer' campaign. It is amazing what you can find in food cupboards. Only buy fresh food and if you need to replace things, buy smaller rather than large packs.

Don't forget to think about what you need to throw away. Whether moving yourself or having removers do it for you, the last thing you want to do is spend time and money moving items you intend to throw away.

ONE TO TWO WEEKS BEFORE

Two weeks before you move, you should have exchanged contracts (page 127). So now you can safely pack more everyday items, but ones that you know you can live without for a couple of weeks – for example, crockery, clothing, CDs, videos and DVDs, alcohol, precious possessions, some bathroom items and all books (bar the ones you are reading, of course). Other items you can start packing include spare bedding, jewellery, pictures and mirrors.

You should also be considering defrosting your freezer as well as having a general clean around the property. This will save you time on the move day – never underestimate just how tiring and time consuming the day itself will be. If you know the cleaning will be a big job or you are too busy to do it yourself, consider hiring someone to do it for you; it will be money well spent.

Finally, if you have pets, children or elderly people staying with you, you'll need to think about what to do about them during the move. It may be more convenient for them to stay for a few days (or at least on the move day) with friends or family.

Moving all your belongings from A to B is stressful in itself without having to worry about anyone that needs extra care. It is much better if they are having fun for the day, rather than being introduced to the new home in chaos and confusion.

Finally make sure you have dropped off or picked up dry cleaning, videos/DVDs and library books, cancelled the milk and newspapers and decided what your last wash will be!

ONE DAY BEFORE

The day before the move, pack everything apart from what you will need for the next day. You might want to pack an overnight bag in case there are any problems on the moving day and your move is delayed. It is also a nice idea to leave a pack of information for your buyer:

- Things that they may need
- Keys labelled
- Where the stopcock is
- Instructions for heating and other appliances

Other useful information to leave could include things like local doctors, dentists, restaurants, local magazines/newspapers and anything else that you think may be helpful.

CHECKLIST OF ITEMS FOR MOVE DAY

Make sure you have easy access to:

✓ Toiletries and other clothes needed for the move day

✓ Breakfast

✓ Cleaning equipment (for where you are moving from and where you are moving to)

✓ Kettle, mugs, tea/coffee, sugar, milk, biscuits

✓ Quick snacks

✓ Water

✓ Cash for any emergencies

✓ Phones and useful numbers (such as the estate agent, removals, legal and utility companies for any last minute calls)

SORTING OUT THE
PAPERWORK

Once you have exchanged contracts it is fairly safe to assume the move is going ahead. Usually your legal advisers will suggest you leave a minimum of two weeks between exchange and completion. This is a good idea. There is a lot you need to organise in addition to the physical move. You have to let everyone know that you are moving and sort out all of your utilities.

Use a checklist so you don't leave anything out. There are some things that you must do before you move and others that can wait until after. While our list is not exhaustive, there are things you should be doing to make the process less stressful and more efficient.

CHANGE OF ADDRESS

A standard letter or printed card may be sufficient. When you are writing to companies to change your address, they will need to know both your old and new address and any account or reference numbers. Addresses connected to insurance or saving policies, bank or savings accounts may need to change. Don't forget a new telephone number may also be required.

- You do not always have to write to a company to change your address details. You may be able to do this by phone, email or by visiting their website and filling in a change of address form.

- **The Post Office** can set up mail redirection. Give as much notice as you can, but they should be able to set this up within ten days. The form can be applied for on-line, by phone or picked up at any local post office. The service can be paid for monthly but can be organised for anything up to a year and renewed for a further year.

- As you receive redirected mail, you can send out a standard letter or card advising that person or company you have changed address.

- **Internet-based companies** can also help. They register your change of address with companies for you. This is a new service, so is not comprehensive. Many government agencies (including the DVLA) will be contacted on your behalf by such

companies. It is important you notify certain departments; otherwise you may be fined.

- The plus side of using such a service is that they can reduce some of the work required. But you may not want to give your bank details to a company (or over the Internet), so even if you do use this service, you may want to contact sensitive organisations (like your bank) yourself.

CHANGING YOUR UTILITIES

A utility company cannot officially change your details until you have confirmed that you are not the owner or, conversely, that you are the new owner of a property. This does not stop you from letting them know you're moving and giving them the new address. Check via your legal adviser whether the new owner will continue with the same utility services.

- You will need someone to read the meters before you leave. Ideally check and agree the meter readings with the new owner on the move day so there is no room for argument at a later date.

- You needn't insist on services being disconnected as this may cause unnecessary costs to the new owner. But you will need to provide the new owner's name so you are not responsible for bills. All utility companies have specialist departments that deal with change of address issues and many have signed up to the change of address services.

MAKING CONTACT

The Post Office
Website: **www.postoffice.co.uk**

Notification for giving change of address:
www.ihavemoved.com

CHECKLIST OF ESSENTIALS FOR CHANGE OF ADDRESS

Who	What to tell them	Helpful information
Minimum of ten days before moving		
Utility companies such as water, gas, electricity, telephone, cable TV and TV licence	Advise them that you have exchanged contracts and inform them of the person who will be responsible for bills. Where necessary, ask them to read the meter and check the reading with them so there are no problems with who owes what when the final bills arrive	Many companies have forms on their websites or special telephone numbers you can call; some have special offers that may save you some money when you move in. Have your account number and a meter reading ready when you call
Post Office	Organise redirection service	Download the form at www.postoffice.co.uk or get a form at a local post office
One week before moving		
Banks and other financial institutions	Send them a standard letter with the information outlined to the right	Include yoiur account number details, your old and new address and when you expect this to take effect
Council (rates, taxes, services)	Send a standard letter and request a statement before you leave	You may be eligible for a refund, so make sure you let them know your new address so they can send you the money
Dentist, vet, optician, any other medical services	Let them know your new address and moving date	They will need to send files to services in the new location, so make sure you have their details with you to give to the same services in the new locality
Car and household and other insurance	Give them your old and new postcode	Your move may affect the cost of your insurance, so make sure you take advantage of any savings
Companies you work for	Let your HR and line manager know your new address and the date of your expected move	This is important if you are leaving your present job; they will need to keep in touch regarding pensions, etc.
Within a week of moving		
Inland Revenue, DVLA, other government departments	They all have their own forms to fill in. For your driving licence, you'll need to fill in a special form and send it to the DVLA or go to your local post office (see www.dvla.gov.uk/coa.htmfor more details)	Do not send your driving licence before you have moved in case you need it for identification purposes or for hiring vehicles

Your new house should feel lighter, more presentable and ready to begin to take on a new personality. You will most likely find that you actually have the space or need for some new things. Remember that whatever you purchase now should be a reflection of the new look you are creating.

most likely things that you always felt needed to be changed or improved, but never got around to doing. Perhaps your old home was no longer meeting the current needs of you and your family. Your new house is waiting to become your new home, your sanctuary and the one place where you truly feel safe and secure. It is where you experience love and intimacy with family and loved ones, entertain friends, relax and rejuvenate your spirits. You now have a clean slate to work with. You are in the ideal situation to put your stamp on every room in your home and make it truly a reflection of yourself and your family.

Although most of what you have is left over from your previous home take advantage of the opportunity to make some changes. Move things around, shake things up, and think creatively.

Unlike my prescriptions for preparing a home for sale such as neutralising, depersonalising and minimising, for long-term living, a home should be a reflection of the personal taste of those who live in it. It should serve the needs of all family members as well as be an aesthetic, harmonious, welcoming and functional environment.

But where do you begin? On the following pages are some room-by-room guidelines to help you settle in to your home quickly so that you will be able to get back to 'normal life' as soon as possible. These guidelines and suggestions should help eliminate some of the confusion that comes from feeling overwhelmed by having to make far too many immediate decisions, as well as help you to avoid making long-term mistakes.

THE PROCESS

Now that the movers have left, don't be daunted by the task ahead of you. The worst is definitely past. Think of this 'settling in' period as an opportunity to reshape your personal world. Relax, put on some inspirational music, pour yourself a drink of whatever makes you feel really good and dive in. Working room by room, it is time to begin to rebuild your interior.

Entrance hall

You never have a second chance to make a first impression. This is where you announce yourself to the world as well as what greets you when open your front door. The feel good factor is critical here. Your entrance should be light and bright, well defined. The style and colours here should be a preview of the rest of the house.

This will introduce your style and ensure that even if you live alone, you'll always be welcomed home.

Key ingredients: plants or flowers, decorative mirror, coat rack or cupboard and pleasant scents. Be sure to include something very personal to you, such as a special rug or runner, artwork, something you collect, or a cherished gift from someone you care about.

Living room

Although there are many different names for the main public room in the home, thinking of it as a 'living room' defines its purpose. This room can be versatile, exactly what you choose to make it, a family gathering place, an 'adults only' room, a place to receive guests, a music room or library. It's whatever suits your personal needs. Once you have decided what you want to do in the room then everything else falls into place. The colours you choose, the furniture and arrangement, floor and window treatment should all enhance this vision.

Key ingredients: Focal point, comfortable seating with conversation groupings, three-tiered lighting (task, accent and ambient) and your prized possessions.

Your living room is the place to showcase those things you are most proud of ... a beautiful antique, special painting, or collection.

Dining room

A separate dining room is a luxury in most homes today. In fact, even if you are fortunate enough to have one, unless you either entertain on a regular basis or have all the space you need in your home, I would suggest giving this room a dual purpose. It could double as a casual family/TV room, home office, library or whatever space you feel your home is lacking. With a little imagination and organisation you can have the best of both worlds. Whatever you decide, for a dining room to fulfil its main purpose there are some things that are a must.

The dining room is where you share your home with those who are closest or most important to you.

Key ingredients: Expandable table and comfortable seating, adequate accessible storage for table settings and linens, serving table or sideboard, chandelier or over table lighting and something beautiful to look at from every side of the table while dining.

Kitchen

The proverbial 'heart of the home' should be functional, but this doesn't mean that you should forget about aesthetics. Colour scheming and co-ordination are just as important here as anywhere. Organisation is key. Use the reach rule: keep everyday items within your natural arm swing. Store articles used weekly at squatting and tip-toe levels. Rarely used items can be stored away, but accessible by using a step stool. Counter tops should remain clutter free and anything visible should be attractively and thoughtfully arranged.

The kitchen is where the health and happiness of the household originate.

Key ingredients: Clean, washable surfaces, built-in storage, eating area for at least two people, adequate and controlled lighting for particular tasks and general ambience, co-ordinated accessories such as crockery, tea towels, place mats and, of course, a touch of greenery (herb plants are always a favourite of mine).

Main bedroom

This is the one place that you can go, shut the door and just get away from it all. Your bedroom, more than any room, should reflect your style, colour palette and needs. Many people try to cram in too many things, like televisions, computers and exercise equipment. I'm a firm believer that your bedroom should only contain those possessions that make you feel good.

Key ingredients: Colour scheme in a favourite shade, a comfortable bed with a headboard, fresh bedding and linens (the best you can afford), light controlling window, dressing table, bedside table and reading lamp, music, personal photographs, mementoes, favourite books and artwork, fresh flowers, candles and plenty of clean fresh air.

Bathroom

The bathroom in any home should be hygienic and functional but it is also a place where you can use the colours, motifs and objects that you love. Its style should be in keeping with the feel of the rest of your house, and if it is an en suite it should be a continuation of the bedroom theme. More than anywhere else in the home, in the bathroom there should be a place for everything and everything in its place.

Key ingredients: Adequate storage, good ventilation and lighting, sufficient towel rails, co-ordinated shower curtain, bath mat, accessories, towels, scented candles, bath salts or essential oils. The bathroom is the one place that you can truly be alone. Take advantage of this. Think of it as your own personal spa.

The bathroom is a place to pamper yourself, relax and recharge your batteries.

Children's rooms

Children's rooms should be age appropriate, yet have the flexibility to be easily adapted to the child's needs as the child grows and matures. Whether the room is for a toddler or a teenager, there are some basic principles that apply across the board. Just as importantly as for an adult, a child should be involved in the décor and function of their own room.

Kids are just newer people. They need scope, yet guidance.

Key ingredients: Storage, storage, and more storage. Because children's rooms often serve dual or multi-functions, adequate storage is required to maintain an organised and functional environment. Built-in or free-standing cupboards, work/study stations, shelving and toy or activity containers help to keep everything in its place. Avoid heavily themed rooms as too soon they will be outgrown. Build in personality with soft furnishings such as bedding and curtains that are easy and inexpensive to change.

Don't try to accomplish everything I've suggested in a day or two. Some things will take longer than others to complete as they require more thought and effort. Remember, 'Rome wasn't built in a day'. Making a house into a home is an ongoing process that is only finished when you move the next time.

TROUBLE SHOOTING

What's your problem?		Who can help you?
Before you move	No time to pack	Removals company (see page 141) Friends and relatives
	Awaiting confirmation of moving dates	Legal company (see page 40)
	Money transfer problems	Legal company or estate agent (see pages 40 and 15)
On the day itself	Buyer is demanding keys to enter the house	Legal company or estate agent (see pages 40 and 15)
	Seller is not moving out fast enough	Legal company (see page 40)
After you have moved	Items left or taken from the property that you did not expect	Estate agent or legal company (see pages 15 and 40)
	Disagreement on utility readings	Relevant utility company (see page 150)

What can be done?

- When briefing removal companies, ask them to quote for their packing service separately. If you get near the move date and have no time, or something unexpected happens, you can weigh up the cost of having everything packed for you.

- Or you can recruit friends and family to help you for a day (there's nothing like a bribe of food and drink). You'll soon get through everything together.

- Your move date (or completion date) is set when you exchange contracts. It then takes approximately ten working days to complete. So if you are days away from exchanging, you can provisionally book your removal (subject to confirmation on exchange).

- If the exchange date keeps moving or it is just not happening, contact your legal company and make them aware that you need to confirm a date in order to book your removal company in time.

- If at exchange or completion one legal company is saying the money has been sent and the recipients have not received it, it might take a couple more hours to go through. Normally a legal company will check its own system regularly and advise you when the money arrives. If it is taking more than a couple of hours for the money to be transferred, get the company responsible for sending the money to check with the bank that the transfer is going through. This should be done via your legal company or the estate agent contacting the buyer's solicitor.

- The buyer can only have the keys if your legal company has confirmed the money has been transferred and you have completed on the sale/purchase. If this has not happened, the buyer has no right to enter the property.

- If you have problems, contact your legal company or estate agent and ask them to help explain this to the purchaser.

- If you have completed on your purchase, you should have access to the property. If the seller is being too slow moving out, talk to them to find out why they are not ready. There may be a valid reason.

- Then call your legal company to find out what is the best course of action to take. If you are likely to incur more costs by moving in late and the seller agrees to pay for this, you may find this to be the best solution.

- If you find that items have been removed or not taken as indicated on the fixtures and fittings forms, then contact the sellers to find out what has happened and try to agree a course of action. The estate agent might act as a go between if needed.

- If you have any further problems, contact your legal company for help.

- Ideally the utility company will have read the meter for you when you move. If you are buying, report the meter reading immediately to the utility company or agree it on the day with the seller and ring it through to the company, then put it in writing and send it to them. If not, Energywatch can arbitrate for you.

- If the dispute continues, the utility company can refer to previous readings and estimate usage. Track the meter readings weekly for four weeks so that you can send evidence of your use. With this information, the utility company should be able to arbitrate the issue fairly.

SECTION FOUR

LETTING A
PROPERTY

Whatever your reason for buying to let, you need to know what to expect. It's the same as normal buying and selling but with added implications. Where will you buy, who will you let the property to? How are you going to finance the venture? How do you manage the on-going finances? What about tax? What responsibilities do you have as a landlord? These and other questions will be answered here.

When considering where and what to invest your money in a buy-to-let, here are some of the questions worth asking the local property experts.

- What influences rental and house prices in this area?
- Are rental and house prices going up or down?
- How much have they increased/decreased since last year?
- What are the monthly average rents of different properties over the last six months or year?
- What types of rent and properties are in short supply?
- What rentals are currently giving the best return on investment?
- Who are the easiest and hardest tenants to find?
- What type of rent/properties are they looking for?
- Who are the most maintenance free tenants?
- Who are renting for long and short term lets and what type of rent/properties do they want?
- Who are the best letting agents?
- Can I apply for any grants to do up properties?
- How much are letting fees?

Another site specifically for landlords is the Residential Landlords Association (see Making contact, previous page), which has information and links that can help you, but you have to pay to use the services.

Once you have researched these sites and found local agents that are members of ARLA, look in the local property papers to see which are both estate agents and letting agents. Good agents should not only be letting agents, but also have an estate agency arm. Ideally look for agents that are members of ARLA and either the NAEA, the Ombudsman Scheme or RICS (see page 168). They should have good coverage with more than one office so that they have people who have knowledge of the whole area you are looking at.

From an agent's perspective, you are potentially a very important source of income. First, you are a cash buyer of property, second, you may spend money with them if you decide to use their letting agency services, and finally, you are likely at some stage to sell the property – now adding to the agent's earnings by giving them your instruction business. So they should be prepared to spend some time helping you to consider different options.

Further research that you can do yourself is watching the property and rental market over a period of time by studying all the local newspapers and answering the questions in the checklist above. It is also useful to chart the purchase price of a property against the rental price in different areas so that you can compare each one to see which is delivering the best return on your purchase price – see chart opposite.

PURCHASE AND RENTAL PRICE COMPARISON (see below left)		
Property	**Average purchase price**	**Average rental price**
1-bed flat		
2-bed flat		
2-bed house		
3-bed house		
4-bed house		

BUY-TO-LET REALITY CHECK

Before you dive into a buy-to-let investment, check what else you could invest your money in and the type of return you would gain.

Although property prices have shot up over the last few years, they could go down. Buying-to-let is a long-term investment and your money will not be easily accessible. So make sure that any money you invest you are not likely to need for some years to come.

Buy-to-let is also a lot of work and it can be expensive if structural work or other defects appear after you have bought the house. If you are only getting a little more out of letting than another investment – such as shares, commodities, bonds or savings scheme – really think through if it is worth the additional hassle and risk.

To help you assess the real profit and loss of any buy-to-let investment you make longer term, there are software packages that you can download from the net or buy on-line (see Making contact, page 168, for one example). They will also help you understand how the financial side of buying-to-let works. Make sure you receive a free demonstration and some references from current clients before you commit to purchase.

Once you have decided to commit your money, make sure you have thoroughly researched your area, property and tenant type and are sure about how to manage being a landlord.

It is not just property information that newspapers can give you. You may be looking for transient people so the job pages can help you assess what type of people may be attracted to the area. You can also write or contact large local employers to ask them if they are likely to have rental needs for the future over and above their current requirements.

MAKING CONTACT

Software package for profit and loss:
www.ezpzsoftware.co.uk/ezpzlord.html
Royal Institute of Chartered Surveyors (RICS)
Website: **www.rics.org.uk**
The Housing Association
Website: **www.housingcorp.co.uk**

The local council planning department or development agencies can offer tremendous amounts of information. For example, they may have plans to regenerate an area and are looking to offer good rates for companies to move there. This may help push up demand for rental properties and, in the longer term, increase property prices. There may be changes to transport links that could improve access to the town centre. A company might be relocating its head office, again increasing demand in the longer term.

Two other sources of information might be your local branch of the Royal Institute of Chartered Surveyors (RICS) and the local Housing Association. RICS has a wealth of information on property, rental and sale prices and research information on the future demand of property in the UK. They may also have sources that can help you locally (see Making contact, above).

Try contacting and talking to your local housing association, too (see also Making contact, above). The association is the main provider of new social housing in the local area. The housing associations currently manage around 1.45 million homes in England alone. Housing associations are run as businesses, but any surplus is ploughed back into the organisation to maintain existing homes and finance new ones. They have information regarding property availability, rental needs and what type of rental properties are in short supply. This information can be shared with the public.

Using these information sources you should have some idea in which areas, property and tenant types you think you might be able to operate a buy-to-let investment. Your research should also have given you an idea of how much properties cost and rent.

Now you are in a position to work out how much money you need to fund your buy-to-let.

FUNDING A BUY-TO-LET
PROPERTY PURCHASE

Funding a property to buy-to-let is different to funding your own home. The key difference is that you need to approach buying to let as a business, throw personal choice and preference out the window and consider carefully how and what you spend money on within the property. You will have to pay the legal and survey fees and stamp duty. Although you can save on contents insurance, you need to have buildings insurance in place when you exchange on a property.

As with buying a property for yourself, your first consideration is to understand the best way for you to fund the purchase. You may have the cash to buy the property outright, or need to part fund and part borrow. You may be able to borrow more money from your existing lender, or you may be able to borrow most of the money through a buy-to-let mortgage.

As this is a business and not a personal purchase, most investors prefer to borrow as much as they can. The reason is that any expenditure on arranging the mortgage, such as advice and fees for securing the loan plus the interest paid on the mortgage, is tax deductible. However you decide to do it, if you borrow you must advise a lender in writing that you intend to buy-to-let. You should take financial advice from an expert in buy-to-let property purchase to discuss the best way.

If you are considering a buy-to-let mortgage, you need to know there are often very different conditions attached versus owning a home yourself. For example, most buy-to-let mortgages require a high deposit level – anything from 15% of the property's value. They may also require evidence that the rental value is achievable and a surveyor and local estate or letting agent would be asked for their views.

There is normally a requirement for the rental value to be up to 50% in excess of the mortgage payments. The reason for this is to ensure you

MAKING CONTACT   Websites with information about
buy-to-let schemes:

www.charcolonline.co.uk
www.moneynet.co.uk
www.financesearch.co.uk

have enough funds to cover the on-going costs of running a property and any lean times if rental prices fall or the property is not let for a period of time.

There are many companies now offering buy-to-let schemes and you can find a range of buy-to-let mortgages at the websites listed in Making contact, above.

Once you have calculated how much you can now afford to pay for a property, you can talk to the local estate and letting agents to help you identify types of properties you can afford as well as the types of tenants you need to target.

RESEARCHING POTENTIAL PROPERTIES

Much of finding and buying property is the same as when buying for your own home. But there is one major difference.

It is important when you are doing this to think about what type of property your tenant would want. The costs for the tenant are the deposit and rent they pay plus utility bills and council tax. Most tenants are also likely to want a property that is easy to clean and a simple garden to care for. Note, too, that they will want a reputable landlord that fixes things in an emergency as well as a property that is well maintained.

A further difference for tenants compared with buyers is that they only rent what they really need. For example, if they only need one bedroom, they will only rent a one-bed property. But when we are buying, we tend to try and afford the best we can, such as a spare room for guests or for new family additions.

You are not buying a property you will live in, but trying to purchase a new asset that will grow in value. You need to purchase a property that

not only gives a good rate of return on the rent, but one which is likely to increase in value in the longer term (see page 164).

As a cash buyer, you can try and secure a good deal via your local estate agent, but it might be worth checking out the local auction house. The latter will give you an idea of the other investors in the market and what they are buying (see page 92). Another type of property to consider is a new build. You may get one with a special deal where the stamp duty or legal fees are paid if you can offer them a quick sale. You may gain a better price by buying off plan (see page 97). Providing you have had a successful survey carried out on the property (see page 119) it should be relatively low maintenance and good for your tenant as new build properties tend to be energy efficient through using the latest building materials. As a result, their gas and electricity bills are lower than older properties.

If you are happy to do some work to the property, you may be able to pick up a bargain by buying a property that needs cosmetic work such as repainting and tidying up. Alternatively if you can take on a property with more work needed – such as a new kitchen or bathroom – this can help enhance the longer-term value of the property. But be aware that you might have to spend time fixing the property before you are able to rent it – and so forego rental income in the short term.

WHO TO LET TO

Some mortgage lenders will not offer buy-to-lets for any tenant, so check before you target a tenant that you can get a buy-to-let mortgage. Once you have researched a list of property types and areas that you can afford to purchase, you can now start confirming the information on rental returns on the different property types in the different areas.

Having narrowed down your areas and property types, you can also start to work out which tenants you are likely to be able to target. This is the final stage in trying to work out which buy-to-let investment is going to give you the best return for your money. There are a variety of tenants that you could target, each will bring its own benefits and drawbacks. The key types of tenants are highlighted below.

STUDENT LETS

These can be good earners as you can rent out many rooms within a property as opposed to the whole property itself. In terms of preparing the property, it does not need to be to a high specification, just hard wearing as this can keep initial costs down.

However, the market tends to be restricted to near the college or university and can be very competitive as other landlords are in the same vicinity. The maintenance expenses can be quite high, too – we all remember what we were like during our college years. The downside is that students are away for long periods during holiday time, bringing your likely rental period down to ten out of twelve months.

LOCAL COUNCIL

It may be worth getting in touch with the local Housing Advice or Housing Benefit office as they can match tenants who may be able to rent privately with benefit help. This can be attractive to landlords, particularly if you do not have time to find tenants or do not want to pay letting agents. The price of the properties tends to be low, too, so you get more properties for your money than in more expensive areas. You also can have rent guaranteed and paid directly from the government/local authority, avoiding collecting rent yourself, but check with your local council how they work. The downside is that in terms of capital appreciation of the property, this may not be as high as for other areas. You do not get to choose the tenant. Some lenders will not lend if you are targeting this clientele.

CORPORATE LETTINGS/PROFESSIONALS

Corporate and professional lets are extremely good in that the people are professionals and their business either supports or pays for the accommodation. Top dollar is paid for good properties that are easy to maintain. You may be able to get an agreement with a business local to you and avoid the finder's fees of letting agents for tenants.

Professional tenants are more likely to want to be in good areas, with good local amenities and transport. A high internal spec will be expected. Both of these can prove expensive in the short term and therefore take longer to pay back, even if they do attract an initial good rental.

PRIVATE TENANTS

Private tenants are a good source of income. The longer you can sign up the tenant for, the more secure your investment is. However, you need to make sure the tenants are credit checked and that you have a solid tenancy agreement in place should anything go wrong. If it is a family, remember that children are more likely to increase the wear and tear of the property. So hard wearing, stain free carpets and a good solid kitchen is critical.

PREPARING **YOUR PROPERTY**

Once you have found a property, you need to ensure that you prepare it well for your prospective tenants. A well-presented property can help ensure it is rented quickly and may even secure you a higher rental price. You should also try and ensure that it is low maintenance and hassle free for you – and your tenant.

First you need to ensure that the utilities work and are safe. This also applies to any electrical appliances you include in the property such as fridge/freezer, dishwasher or kettle. Do not forget that all electric lights and sockets need to be tested for safety.

For the gas, a CORGI registered engineer must carry out the inspection and safety check and give you a certificate. This is a legal requirement under The Gas Safety (Installation and Use) Regulations 1998. You also need these to be checked regularly and in the case of gas, annually.

If the property was built after 1982, legally under The Buildings Regulations 1991 Act it must have a smoke alarm. Whatever the age of your property, it is advisable for you to fit one or more in your buy-to-let, just in case.

For information about CORGI registered engineers see Making contact, opposite. Also included in the box is a website for organising gas and electrical safety checks and the required certificates. These cost around £100 but it is a tax-deductible expense.

If you decide to rent your property furnished or have any furnishings in the

MAKING CONTACT

CORGI registered engineers:
Website: **www.corgi-gas.com**

Gas and electrical safety checks:
Website: **www.gesc.co.uk**

property, you also need to ensure that you comply with The Furniture and Furnishings (Fire and Safety) Regulations 1988. These state that all upholstered furniture with a filling material must have a permanent sewn in label, which shows it satisfies the regulations.

When re-decorating the property, the paintwork should have fresh and neutral tones. Ideally, look for paint that is easy to clean and keep some spare just in case it needs a fresh coat at a later date.

Any improvements that you make to a property need to be cost effective and hard wearing. Remember that only money spent on maintaining, not improving, the property will be tax deductible. It is advisable to research carefully any kitchen and bathroom fittings, as you want ones that will last. Not only do they need to be hard wearing, but try and avoid highly fashionable looks as these date quickly.

There is no point spending tens of thousands of pounds on items which only last a few years. It is better, instead, to spend a few thousand pounds on good quality fitting that you can afford to update every few years.

Do spend on fans for both the kitchen and any bathrooms to avoid moisture damage and build-up of unpleasant odours.

Before you buy, consider what happens if fixture or fittings are damaged. For example, would a new drawer, top or unit in a kitchen be easily replaceable or would you have to replace the entire unit? Fitted items such as a fridge or freezer tend to cost more if built-in. So if they break or leak it may be more cost effective to spend on freestanding versions.

With carpets, these are likely to need replacing often, so consider buying stain resistant, neutral carpets as well as some spare remnants. If possible, choose from ones that will be easy to replace.

Instead of curtains, which could be considered high maintenance, consider blinds, which are easier to clean and replace.

Make sure you keep receipts for everything you buy. You can claim tax relief on essential maintenance, but not on improvements.

LETTING YOUR **PROPERTY**

CHECKLIST OF THINGS TO DO WHEN FINDING A TENANT AND LETTING A PROPERTY

✓ Advertise for a tenant
✓ Show potential tenants around
✓ Check interested tenants credit and references
✓ Issue and agree on the tenancy terms
✓ Organise taking the deposit and rent
✓ Insure yourself and make sure the tenant is insured too
✓ Inventory check
✓ Handle and retain the deposit
✓ Collect the rent
✓ Keep the property maintained
✓ Organise the annual safety check

While an agent takes care of all the work, bear in mind their services cost you money – keep a close eye on what you receive and any deductions that are made.

Now that your property is ready to let, you need to make a decision as to whether you are going to handle all or part of the letting yourself or hand over to a lettings specialist. Most letting agents offer two levels of service. First, a tenant finding service where they can organise everything up until the time the tenants move in. Or they will fully manage the property, including collecting and sending you the rent and basic property maintenance. Any major maintenance usually requires your permission, but they will normally organise this for you too.

When choosing a letting agent, ensure they are a member of the Association of Residential Letting Agents (ARLA) (see page 165) as this is an unregulated market. ARLA agents have to hold professional indemnity insurance and be in business for more than two years. As members of the association they are also given regular updates on the latest legal or regulatory requirements.

It is advisable to shop around for the different services offered. The costs can vary between a flat fee, 50% of the first month's rent to 10% of the full rental income over the rental term. Fees for fully managing your property range on average from 10% to 15% of the monthly rental income. Do not forget to negotiate this as low as possible as, in most areas, agents are competing heavily for your business. Remember that these fees are tax deductible.

When choosing a letting agent, look for the same things as for an estate agent (page 15). In fact, many estate agents also run a lettings division. Depending on the level of competition in the area, letting tends to be more profitable, so the service offered should be better.

TYPES OF
TENANCY AGREEMENT

If you decide to be paid weekly you need to provide a written record such as a rent book to the tenant.

The legal requirements of letting and renting a property are fundamental to a successful relationship and the money you make. We only ever rely on the legal documents when we have a problem to solve. For example, if the tenant is not paying their rent, you need to cancel the agreement, or if the tenant is not looking after the home properly and you need to take action.

Your letting agent will normally have tenancy agreements that you can use or purchase and they should spend time going through the different agreements with you.

You could create your own version or buy one off the shelf from a legal stationers or sites such as those listed in the Making contact box, page 178. It is advisable to seek help or final approval from a letting agent or specialist solicitor for your individual circumstances.

Any agreement you use should cover both your and the tenant's details and what you have agreed. This should include such things as your name and the tenant's, the address of the property, the date the tenancy starts and ends and the amount of deposit and rent you have agreed. Do not forget that you need to agree a date each month of when and how you will be paid.

MAKING CONTACT

Websites for buying a tenancy agreement:
www.Lawpack.co.uk
www.landlordlaw.co.uk
www.rentamatic.co.uk

In the contract there will need to be provision for an acceptable timeframe in which to give notice of termination and what happens at the termination stage. For example, what checks are required for the deposit to be given back to the tenant. You also need to add in anything else that you agreed such as items you are supplying for the tenant's use.

When deciding on which type of tenancy agreement you will have, first you ought to check which one your lender will approve. Although there are several types of agreement and you can create your own, the main one used in the private rental sector and approved by lenders is the assured short-hold tenancy.

ASSURED SHORT-HOLD TENANCY

Introduced in 1989, the assured short-hold tenancy agreement is the one most often required or requested by lenders. The reason why lenders like this type of agreement is that it reduces their (and your) risk. Whatever happens during the agreement period, the tenant only has the right to stay in the property until the end of the agreement or if there are issues, for a maximum of six months. After that, the landlord has the right to take back possession of the property or offer a new agreement that may have the rent changed. By signing the agreement, the tenant is committed to pay the rent for the agreed time period of the term.

The majority of tenancies are set for twelve months. However, you can also have short-term lets that are typically less than one year. The latter tend to attract a higher rental value, because you need to replace tenants more often (and therefore incur more costs tenant finding). Do not forget that the legal fees and costs are tax deductible.

ORGANISING THE LET FOR A TENANT

Once you or your letting agent has found a tenant, there are various costs and responsibilities associated with organising the letting to the tenant. Many letting agents will include these checks as part of their 'finding a tenant' service, even if you are not using them to manage your property. Alternatively you can do them yourself.

The first of these are checks that are made on the tenant to ensure they can pay the rent. Typically they include credit references and references from employers regarding their income level. The letting agent can help with this, whether you are using them to manage the property or not and will also advise on companies that can do this for you. Alternatively the main sites that we have mentioned have links to companies which will do credit checks costing from £35 per person. These fees are tax deductible.

The next check is an inventory. An independent party is best placed to do this. It is an important job as it records the condition of the property and any contents owned by the landlord at the start and the finish of the tenancy. Apart from noting natural wear and tear over time, if the tenant has mistreated or damaged the property in any way, the inventory checks give you recourse to withhold or make good the damage at the tenant's cost before you give them back any of their deposit. Inventories cost from £15 an hour to create and could cost up to £100 per check. It is usual practice to share the cost of the inventory with the tenant, paying for one check each.

You can register on-line and keep an up-to-date list of an inventory using the website www.inventory manager.co.uk. Any inventory fees are tax deductible.

RUNNING A BUY-TO-LET

The main decision to be made is whether you wish to run the property yourself or hand over the vast majority of the responsibility to the letting agent. Your choice determines how much it will cost you on-going and what you will need to do to run your investment successfully.

Making sure you have budgeted for insurance, maintenance and any other extras will help to avoid surprise costs that may turn your investment into a loss.

Over and above the costs of the letting agent, you will also need to pay for insurance and maintenance. It is impossible to give 'average' figures on these costs as they depend on the property, the tenant, the length of time the property is let for and the area you are letting in.

INSURANCE

Taken out over and above the normal buildings insurance on the property, this covers you for things such as periods when the property is empty, if there are problems with the tenant paying their rent, or for any legal expenses you may incur when trying to secure vacant possession.

Although you will need a specific quote for this, costs start from around £50 per property per year and are tax deductible.

MAINTENANCE

This will vary dramatically depending on the type of property you are letting. Due to changes in the law, it is the landlord's responsibility to provide a safe environment for electricity and gas. You even need to ensure that properties are protected by a mains operated interlinked smoke alarm. Annual checks need to be organised and paid for.

As a landlord, you will also be responsible for maintenance of the physical fixtures and fittings. These are items such as drainage, water, electricity and gas. If something goes wrong within the flat, such as a leak that causes damage, the tenant is liable only if they were at fault. If these are classed as essential expenditure, they are tax deductible.

EXTRAS

Depending on your agreement with your tenant, as a landlord you pay items such as ground rent or service/maintenance charges, particularly on

YOUR RESPONSIBILITIES

As a landlord there are several regulations you need to abide by. It is important you understand them as you may be liable for fines or even be sent to prison if you break the law. Leader, the UK's largest independently owned letting agents, produce the following list of responsibilities:

1 **Property must meet with** the building standard regulations set out under your local council's guidelines. You can get these from the Environmental Health Department at your local council.

2 **Repairs to and safety of the structure** of the property, any hot water installations, water supply; all sanitary and drainage installations; lighting, heating, ventilation and any damp problems.

3 **Landlords must allow their tenants 'quiet enjoyment'** of their property for the period of the tenancy, giving at least 24 hours written notice before a visit (bar emergencies).

4 **Adhere to gas and furniture and furnishings regulations** and ensure all electrical systems and landlord owned appliances are safe to use, including toaster, kettle, washing machine, microwaves, cookers, dishwashers etc and that instructions for use are given for each one.

5 **Have mains operated smoke detectors** installed on each floor in all residential buildings built after June 1992.

6 **Provide a contact address in the UK** or a UK address which the tenant could serve notice of proceedings should the need arise.

7 **To have Tenancy Agreements stamped** within 30 days of the start date of the tenancy. It is an offence under Section 15 of the Stamp Act 1891 not to do this. Unstamped Tenancy Agreements may not be accepted as evidence in a Civil Court.

8 **Not to discriminate against** a tenant because of their sex, race, religion or disability. This is laid down in the Sex Discrimination Act 1975, the Race Relations Act 1976 and the Disability Discrimination Act 1995.

You are unlikely to gain any tax allowance for improvements to the property, but you may receive help from the local council or housing authority if they offer grants to bring properties back into use.

a flat. The tenant is responsible for connection and disconnection of utilities and for the utility bills. They are also liable for council tax and insurance of their own belongings.

Although the above responsibilities may appear to involve huge amounts of costs, a buy-to-let needs to be treated as a business so many of the costs incurred are off set against any gains you make and therefore can reduce your tax liability.

The main costs that are considered deductible are items that are considered necessary costs for running the property. These include many of the items mentioned above such as letting management fees, insurance, maintenance costs and any service costs you incur such as gardening or cleaning.

MAKING A COMPLAINT

The main problems that can arise when buying to let for landlords (and tenants) are, first, at the beginning of the letting process making sure that the tenant has been thoroughly checked either by the landlord or by the letting agent. Secondly at the time when the tenants 'check in' and finally when they 'check out'.

TENANT CHECKS

It is critical that you or a letting agent make the necessary checks on a tenant as you are letting someone into your property to live. The checks are:

1 Identity
2 Their ability to pay the deposit and rent
3 That they will look after the property and anything you own left in the property.

To make these checks thoroughly, you will need to pay out for credit and reference checks, qualifying the source of both. A good letting agent should be used to the pitfalls that can occur during these checks and have methods to ensure they are accurate and true.

If you are using a letting agent and feel the above has not been done and you are having problems as a result, make sure they are a member of ARLA (see Making contact opposite). Check they have adhered to the practices laid out by either organisation and discuss the issues first with the agent. If you are not happy with the response, you can contact the relevant organisation for further assistance. At worst you may need to consult your legal company if you feel the need to take further action.

SIGNING THE AGREEMENT

To try to avoid any area of confusion or doubt, go through the agreement with the tenant, paragraph by paragraph.

- Ask the tenant to sign or initial every page to confirm they have read and understood each one. If there are any disputes over the agreement later, this shows you did thoroughly check this

with the tenant before they signed. A good letting agents should do this for you.

CHECKING THE PROPERTY'S CONDITION

You must have this recorded prior to the tenant moving in – don't leave it for a few days! To avoid potential future problems, do the following:

- Never use an old inventory, always start a fresh one. An independent check is best so that no one is doing it with their own interest at heart.

- Agree that wear and tear will take place during the tenancy, but that when the tenant departs you will be looking to highlight stains on carpets or badly chipped or cracked areas around the property, which would mean paying out unnecessarily for additional work to be done. This is partly what the deposit is there to cover.

- Take photos at the time of inventory too. Not just of the good areas of the property, but also of areas that have a problem, so that you do not forget a year down the line that it existed.

- To avoid potential problems with misuse of equipment (such as a dishwasher or oven) show the tenant how to use it on the day they move in and make sure they have the instruction books to hand too.

The inventory needs to be done thoroughly on the way in and on the way out and ensure you or an independent inventory person makes a note of all of everything listed above – preferably with the tenant there too. On the way in it is crucial to have the information on the condition of the property and the

MAKING CONTACT

Service	Who to complain to/ seek advice from	Telephone	Email	Website
Tenants				
	Independent Housing Ombudsman	020 7836 3630	ombudsman@ihos.org.uk	www.ihos.org.uk
Letting agents				
	Association of Residential Letting Agents (ARLA)	0845 345 5752	info@arla.co.uk	www.arla.co.uk
	National Approved Letting Scheme (NALS)	01242 581712	info@nalscheme.co.uk	www.nalscheme.co.uk

items left, so that on the way out, deposits can be returned quickly to the tenant (they may need the money to put down another deposit) or fairly withheld if problems occur. If you do have a dispute, this should be helpful to clarify who is right and wrong. Alternatively, people and organisations who can help are:

- The letting agent and inventory person, who should be able to do this fairly and arbitrate an amicable result
- Any of the organisations highlighted above. The Independent Housing Ombudsman Scheme offer an independent arbitration for when landlords and tenants cannot resolve disputes between them
- The Citizens Advice Bureau (see page 55).

LETTING AGENTS

There are many problems that may arise from working with letting agents. Some of the main ones that might occur are:

- Being slow at forwarding you rental monies
- Giving prospective tenants keys to your property rather than accompanying the viewing
- Not taking responsibility for sorting out property problems when they are supposed to be fully managing for you.

To avoid these and other problems, make sure your agent is a member of ARLA or NALS (see above). Their members have to abide by a code of conduct. If you think they are falling below these standards and are not happy that your concerns are being resolved effectively, you can contact ARLA for help. Both of these organisations have their own arbitration procedures.

RESPONDING TO TENANT QUERIES

As a landlord, it is critical that you – or the managing agent – respond to tenant queries as fast as possible. Not doing so is the worst possible thing you can do to a tenant.

- You want them to take care of your property, so if they highlight a problem or have a query, the quicker you deal with it the better. If your tenants feel you are taking care of them, they are more likely to take care of your property.
- If there is a serious problem with something such as a leaking washing machine or boiler, you are likely to be the person to pick up the tab on any long-term damage, so deal with it as quickly as possible.
- You have a duty to the tenant on electrics and gas (see page 180) to ensure they are safe.

One of the ways to avoid these issues (and prevent you having to sort out night-time emergencies!) is to use a competent letting agent. They should have a list of respectable, qualified and checked companies to solve any emergency or other issues that arise in your property. This can make a big difference to the costs and time you have to spend on your property, which otherwise might be wasted on someone you do not know or have just picked out at random from a telephone book.

TROUBLE SHOOTING

Before and after getting a tenant

What's your problem?	Who can help you?
Can't get a tenant	Letting agent (see page 176)
Tenant is not paying	Letting agent (see page 176) Legal company (see page 40) Association of Residential Letting Agents (see page 165)
Tenant is damaging the property	Letting agent (see page 176) Legal company (see page 40)
Tenant is not moving out	Letting agent (see page 176) Legal company(see page 40)
Letting agent is not managing the property	Letting agent (see page 176) Association of Residential Letting Agents (see page 165) Residential Landlord Associations (see page 165)
Property is not let for a long period	Insurance company (see page 180)

What can be done?

- If you are not getting any interest in the property, something is wrong. It might be price, location or to whom you are targeting the property. Talk to a local letting agent to find out why the problem exists.
- If you are already working with one, talk to them as to why they think you are not getting people to view. You may need to consider changing agent.
- If you have interest but no one is making an offer, then you need to know what these people are eventually renting. Talk to them to find out why they did not take your property and what they thought was wrong with it. Also ask what others are offering that makes their property more attractive than yours.

- If you are managing the tenant yourself, you need to write to the tenant to advise that they owe you money.
- If you are a member of the Residential Landlord Association or Association of Residential Letting Agents, they are a good place to turn to for initial advice, most of which will be free.
- If the tenant still does not pay, you need to contact your legal company for the best advice and action. Make sure you put everything in writing and keep a chronological list of dates and times you contacted the tenant, including responses from all parties.

- Take photographs of the damage that has been done and provide evidence from your inventory report that this was not damaged before the tenant arrived.
- Write to the tenant advising the cost of repair and replacement and try to come to an amicable solution.
- If you are unhappy about the tenant continuing to live in the property, read through the contract and, if necessary, contact your legal company to advise you on how to evict the tenant.

- You need help from the legal company or letting agent if the property is being managed. It is not easy to get someone evicted without force so try to resolve the issue(s) as soon as possible, before it gets out of hand.

- When you are paying for the agent to manage the property and he/she cannot find a tenant, they are not running the relevant checks on tenants and on the property, or not transferring rent to you quickly then you need to check your agreement with them and their membership of one of the organisations described on page 183.
- Write to the company with your concerns or meet with them and agree in writing what will happen as a result.
- Look for breaches in your contract that allow you to change your letting agent. Advise your tenant of the change.

- Don't forget that you may have taken out insurance to cover this issue. Contact the insurance company for a claim form and take the action outlined above in 'Can't get a tenant'.

GLOSSARY OF TERMS

Bid price: The offer price that you make on a property in Scotland.

Buying off plan: Purchase of a new home from the 'plans' before it is built.

Capital gains tax: Tax by the government on any profit you make from the sale of certain assets.

Commission fee: A fee that is based on a percentage of the final selling price of a home. For example, if the commission fee is 1% and the property is sold for £100,000 then the commission fee will be .01 × £100,000 = £1000.

Commonhold: A 'title' being introduced with new legislation on leasehold properties. It refers to a new form of tenure for flat owners or companies created by tenants to manage the common parts of the flats.

Comparables: Sales particulars or examples of properties sold that are similar to or the same as the property you are looking at selling or buying.

Contract completion: When the buyer takes legal ownership of the new property – typically the same day you move in.

Contract exchange: When legal companies confirm that the seller and buyer's contracts have both been signed and confirm the date for completion.

Conveyancing: Description of the legal work for buying and selling a property.

Deeds: Proof of ownership of the property, which is usually held by the mortgage lender.

Deposit monies: The money that you need to pay at time of exchange. Typically it ranges from 5 to 10%, but can be set at any level the buyer and seller agree.

Disbursements: The charges the legal company incurs when carrying out their conveyancing and which are passed directly onto you. For example, local search or mortgage valuation fees.

Endowment: A saving scheme that is used primarily to pay off a mortgage.

Fixtures and fittings: The items at a property that are attached to walls, floors, ceilings and doors. Examples are light switches, kitchen units, door handles, lampshades, outside lights.

Freehold: The ownership of land and property until it is sold.

Instruction: When an agent gains a property to sell.

Interest only mortgage: A type of mortgage where you only pay interest on the amount borrowed.

Joint tenancy: Where you own the property jointly with another person and, irrespective of the will, will pass to the survivor on death.

Leasehold: The ownership of land or property for a set period of time.

Loan-to-value ratio: The percentage amount of money you borrow on a mortgage versus the total cost of the property you purchase. For example, if you buy a property for £100,000 and have a mortgage of £80,000, the Loan-to-value ratio is 80%.

Local searches: Information gained from the local council on planning matters and some environmental factors that may effect your property purchase. Your legal company sends off for these when you are buying a property and they report on issues such as transport plans and flooding.

Mortgage agreement in principle (MAP): A letter confirming that, 'in principle', a mortgage lender is willing to lend a certain level of money whether a property has been found or not.

Mortgage indemnity insurance: An insurance policy taken out by the lender to cover them if you default on mortgage payments. Normally it applies to mortgages that are higher than a 90%

loan-to-value ratio. However, the cost is passed on to you, the lendee.

Mortgage redemption penalties: An amount that lenders charge if you redeem your mortgage earlier than contractually agreed.

Mortgage roll number or mortgage reference number: The reference number used to identify your mortgage account.

Multiple agency: An agreement where you instruct more than one estate agent to sell your property.

Negative equity: When the price of a property falls below the value of the loan borrowed against it. For example, if you originally purchase a property for £100,000 and have an £80,000 mortgage, but then the market price of the property drops to £75,000, the negative equity is £5000.

Office copy entries: Copies of the Land Registry title of a property.

Part exchange : When you sell your property to a builder in return for one of their new properties.

Planning permission: Required when changes are made to properties such as an extension or erection of a new building. Planning applications need to be made to the local council planning office.

Property portal: Internet sites that have lots of property from different agents. Examples are www.rightmove.co.uk or www.asserta.co.uk

Repayment mortgage: A mortgage where your monthly payments are high enough to pay off interest on the monies you have borrowed and repay the loan at the same time.

Restrictive covenant: A legal document that places a restriction on what can be done to a property. For example, if the property has lots of land, it may be sold with a restrictive covenant that stops anyone from building on the land.

Sales particulars: The details produced by estate agents on a property they are selling. They have a summary of the property, details of the number of rooms, their sizes and the location of the property.

Sole agency: An agreement that instructs one estate agent only to sell your property.

Stamp duty: A levy paid on completion of contracts. It is based on the value of the property and is charged at a percentage level. For example, a 1% stamp duty is applied to all properties bought up to £60,000.

Subject to contract: Properties are said to be 'sold subject to contract' when an offer has been accepted on a property and there is no exchange or completion of contracts.

Tenents in common: Where two or more people purchase a property, the ownership can be split to reflect the amount of deposit or the amount of mortgage payments they will be making. For example, a property purchased for £100,000 where one person is paying 70% of the costs might own 70% of the property. Their share is also passed according to their Will, not automatically to the surviving owner.

Title: Every property and the attached land is registered at the Land Registry by law. Every property or land purchased is given a 'Title' as a reference.

Valuation: Used for several descriptions in the property world. An estate agent will offer a 'free valuation', which is the price they believe a property should be marketed and sold for. A lender will carry out a 'mortgage valuation', which you pay for, to establish that the property is as described on your mortgage application form. A surveyor will give a valuation on a property having carried out a paid for Home Sale and Valuation or Buildings survey.

Vendor: The person who is selling a property.

ABBREVIATIONS

BBR: Bank base rate

CCJ: County Court judgement

DG: Double glazing

DVLA: Drivers Vehicle Licensing Agency

GFCH: Gas fired central heating

GVW: Gross vehicle weight

HSV: Home sale and valuation

PVC: Plasticised polyvinyl chloride (refers to the type of windows in the property)

SUDG: Secondary double glazing

SVR: Standard variable rate

UPVC: Unplasticised polyvinyl chloride (refers to the type of windows in the property)

INDEX

Acknowledgements

The publishers wish to thank the following people and organisations for their help with the creation of this book:

Kate Faulkner

Nikki English

Margie Lindsay

Ian Tuttle

Andrew Gilbert of Winkworth, 5/6 Station Buildings,
Ealing Common, London W5 3NU

Simon Ginsburg and everybody at Kew Riverside Park,
Bessant Drive, Kew, London

Louise Everritt and everybody at Laing Homes, Langdon
Park Complex, Kingston Road, Teddington

David Hayward and everybody at Channel 5 for all
their help with pictures

Katherine, Trisha, Russell and everybody at
Putney Wharf, 212–214 Putney Bridge Road,
London SW15 2NA

Karen Babington   www.easier2move.co.uk

Alistair Kinnear   www.surveysonline.co.uk

Mark Spurling   RBS Associates

Alan Thurlow   www.leaders.co.uk

The NAEA, The Ombudsman, RICS, Hometrack and
Abbey National

Sarah Lee and Fiona Smith, Fulham Sports & Spinal
Physiotherapy Clinic, Swan Mews, Parsons Green Lane,
London SW6 4QT

All photographs are by Nikki English with the exception of those on the following pages, which are by Chris Ridley:
35, 36, 37, 38, 39, 155, 156, 157